DAVID WILLIAMSON is Australia's best known and most widely performed playwright. His first full-length play *The Coming of Stork* was presented at La Mama Theatre in 1970 and was followed by *The Removalists* and *Don's Party* in 1971. His prodigious output since then includes *The Department, The Club, Travelling North, The Perfectionist, Sons of Cain, Emerald City, Top Silk, Money and Friends, Brilliant Lies, Sanctuary, Dead White Males, After the Ball, Corporate Vibes, Face to Face, The Great Man, Up For Grabs, A Conversation, Charitable Intent, Soulmates, Birthrights, Amigos, Flatfoot, Operator, Influence, Lotte's Gift, Scarlet O'Hara at the Crimson Parrot, Let the Sunshine*; *Rhinestone Rex and Miss Monica, Don Parties On*, a sequel to *Don's Party*; *At Any Cost?* (co-written with Mohamed Khadra), *Nothing Personal, When Dad Married Fury, Managing Carmen, Happiness, Rupert* and *Cruise Control*.

His plays have been translated into many languages and performed internationally, including major productions in London, L.A., New York and Washington. *Dead White Males* completed a successful UK Production in 1999. *Up For Grabs* went on to a West End production starring Madonna in the lead role. In 2008 *Scarlet O'Hara at the Crimson Parrot* premiered at the Melbourne Theatre Company starring Caroline O'Connor and directed by Simon Phillips.

As a screenwriter, David has brought to the screen his own plays including *The Removalists, Don's Party, The Club, Travelling North* and *Emerald City* along with his original screenplays for feature films including *Libido, Petersen, Gallipoli, Phar Lap, The Year of Living Dangerously* and *Balibo*. The adaptation of his play *Face to Face*, directed by Michael Rymer, won the Panavision Spirit Award for Independent Film at the Santa Barbara International Film Festival.

David was the first person outside Britain to receive the George Devine Award (for *The Removalists*). His many awards include 12 Australian Writers' Guild AWGIE Awards, five Australian Film Institutes' Awards for Best Screenplay and, in 1996 The United Nations Association of Australia Media Peace Award. In 2005 he was awarded the Richard Lane Award for services to the Australian Writers' Guild. David has received four honorary doctorates and been made an Officer of the Order of Australia.

David has been named one of Australia's Living National Treasures.

Also by David Williamson

A Conversation
After The Ball
A Handful of Friends
Amigos
At Any Cost?
Birthrights
Brilliant Lies
Charitable Intent
Corporate Vibes
Dead White Males
Don's Party
Emerald City
Face to Face
Flatfoot
Influence
Jugglers Three
Let the Sunshine
Managing Carmen
Money and Friends
Nothing Personal
Operator
Rhinestone Rex and Miss Monica
Rupert
Sanctuary
Scarlett O'Hara at the Crimson Parrot
Siren
Sons of Cain
Soulmates
The Club
The Coming of Stork
The Department
The Great Man
The Perfectionist
The Removalists
Third World Blues
Top Silk
Travelling North
Up for Grabs
What If You Died Tomorrow?
When Dad Met Fury

MONEY & FRIENDS

David Williamson

Currency Press • Sydney

CURRENCY PLAYS

First published in 1992 by Currency Press Pty Ltd
Gadigal Land, Suite 310, 46-56 Kippax Street, Surry Hills, NSW 2010, Australia
enquiries@currency.com.au; www.currency.com.au

Reprinted 1997, 2014, 2024.

The Cataloguing-in-Publication data for this title is available from the National Library of Australia.

Printed by Fineline Print + Copy Service, Revesby, NSW

Cover design by Trevor Hood

Currency Press acknowledges the Traditional Owners of the Country on which we live and work. We pay our respects to all Aboriginal and Torres Strait Islander Elders, past and present.

Contents

regional n

INDUSTRIAL SHARE LIST

Up to close of b

MINING AN

Celebrating friendship

Aubrey Mellor

RQTC, Queensland's State Theatre Company, celebrated its twenty-first year with a production of David Williamson's latest play - twenty-one years after Melbourne's La Mama Theatre produced his first play, *The Coming of Stork*, in 1970.

Money and Friends is a departure from the semi-autobiographical plays such as *Emerald City*. Always timely, David now reminds us of the value of friendship in our materialistic world. Set at the coastal retreat of Crystal Inlet, the characters move from deck to deck of their holiday houses. The decks, suspended between sea and land, a metaphorical no-man's land between their public and private worlds. At the heart of this community of friends is deep tristesse. Two lonely characters are in grief and bitterness at the loss of their partners --- Margaret and Peter now fulfil a need in each other's lives with their genuine friendship, made all the more interesting because it is between man and woman. Other characters in the play are married but not friends --- these two are friends but not married. The difficulty of maintaining friendship within marriage is a recurrent theme in many of David's plays. In this play, friendships are tested, not just by money, but by truth.

'The Awfuls' as Robyn Nevin fondly dubbed the other characters in the play, have never been quite that to me. From the early drafts through to the published script, David has always drawn them with wry affection. He sees their follies and understands them every bit as much as his central characters. They are, after all, a product of their society. and as Peter says, 'Their fallibility makes them more endearing.' Where the playwright is unforgiving is in their truly awful behaviour --- their ultimately selfish acts when the chips are down.

On the other hand, Margaret, the historian, is one of the most interesting women Williamson has created. Her brusque and forceful personality is a survival mechanism. Judging by audience response to the play's commentary on the limited sexual opportunities for older women compared to those available to men, this new theme of David's has found its mark. As Margaret points out, 'a man can marry someone twenty years younger and nobody bats an eyelid' but without the approval of her friends Margaret is unable to maintain a relationship with any of her liasons.

David Williamson has created characters who are recognisable but not stereotypical, who evoke immediate sympathy and response with audiences. *Money and Friends* is certainly destined to become one of his most debated and enduring plays.

Sydney, December 1991

A reckless, passionate affair ...

Robert Gottliebsen

Despite the abundance of land, Australians have traditionally treasured property ownership. Much of the wealth generated in the country has come from sustained rises in the value of houses, farms and commercial real estate. But periodically our nation converts the traditional financial attraction of property into a reckless, passionate love affair. During these 'affairs', property buyers believe that they have discovered the ultimate source of wealth; an asset that will go up in value but never down. Greed takes over and they want as much of this wealth as they can get and so are prepared to borrow extraordinary sums to over-indulge the property passion.

Probably the biggest property boom in our history took place in the 1880s. Australians discovered in the 1890s that property can indeed fall dramatically and many were wiped out. In the decades that followed we had many booms and busts but none was as big as the 1880s --- that is until 100 years later in the 1980s.

The collapse of so many savings institutions in the 1890s led Australia into strong controls of the banking system for most of the twentieth century. This led to a very protected banking environment where skills in evaluating customers and loan securities were not highly developed. Many of these controls were released in the 1980s and at the same time, sixteen overseas banks were invited to move into the Australian market. The existing banks defended their market share against the newcomers and the expanding State government owned banks and the result was a huge rise in the amount of credit available. Few people realised that many key bank executives did not have the knowledge to cope with the changed situation. A great many covered their lack of business understanding by loaning on the asset they felt most comfortable with --- property. In the 1980s it was possible to borrow almost 100% of the value of a property because bankers could not conceive of it falling --- there was so much latent demand. Bankers usually insisted on personal guarantees but it was very common to regard them as a formality, given that the loan itself was secured on an asset that could not fall in value and was likely to rise sharply. The bankers and their clients had not remembered history. But then the Treasurer of the day, Paul Keating, decided to slow the economy down using high interest rates. Keating knew that if he over-shot he would cause a recession but was confident he had the ability to slow down the economy without causing long term damage. In *Business Review Weekly*, July 14, 1989 he declared that he would try and smash the property market. Few people took much notice --- after all, it was 'not possible for property to fall'. For a long time it seemed no-one was listening to Keating's slow down message and so he had to raise interest rates much higher than he had previously anticipated. Worse still, he and the Canberra bureaucrats did not understand the damage they were doing, not only to the property market but to the owners of good businesses that had borrowed money from the bankers. The end result of the prolonged high interest rates was the most severe recession for sixty years. Banks lost a fortune. Many bank executives lost their jobs. Many panicked when they saw property falling and sold up the security held by hapless clients and called on the personal guarantees. This sent the property market even lower, sparking off other failures. The dreams of fabulous wealth were only memories for those sitting in the bankruptcy courts. It will be a long time before the lesson that property can fall in value is forgotten, but the nature of Australians is such, that sometime in the 21st century, once again, property will lure Australians into reckless investing helped by bankers who will have forgotten history.

Robert Gottliebsen
Chairman and Editorial Director
BRW Publications
Melbourne, 1991

Money and Friends was first performed on 28 November, 1991 by the Royal Queensland Theatre Company at Brisbane's Suncorp Theatre with the following cast:

MARGARET	Robyn Nevin
PETER	John Gaden
CONRAD	Don Barker
JAQUIE	Caroline Kennison
STEPHEN	Peter Carroll
PENNY	Barbara Stephens
ALEX	Brandon Burke
VICKI	Sally McKenzie
JUSTIN	Paul Bishop

Directed by Aubrey Mellor
Designer, Dale Ferguson
Lighting Designer, David Walters

The playwright and director thank Wayne Harrison for his invaluable dramaturgical assistance.

All photographs are from the RQTC production, 1991. Photographer: Sesh Raman. *Cover*: Robyn Nevin as Margaret and John Gaden as Peter. *Page vi*: Robyn Nevin as Margaret, Barbara Stephens as Penny and John Gaden as Peter. *Page 17*: Above: John Gaden as Peter and Robyn Nevin as Margaret. Below: Sally McKenzie as Vicki. *Page 33*: Robyn Nevin as Margaret and John Gaden as Peter. *Page 39*: John Gaden as Peter and Barbara Stephens as Penny. *Page 43*: Robyn Nevin as Margaret and Paul Bishop as Justin. *Page 57*: John Gaden as Peter, Brandon Burke as Alex and Sally McKenzie as Vicki. *Page 61*: Above: John Gaden as Peter and Brandon Burke as Alex. Below: Sally McKenzie as Vicki and Brandon Burke as Alex. *Page 69*: Above: Caroline Kennison as Jaquie, Don Barker as Conrad, Robyn Nevin as Margaret, Sally McKenzie as Vicki, Brandon Burke as Alex, Peter Carroll as Stephen and Barbara Stephens as Penny. Below: Peter Carroll as Stephen, Barbara Stephens as Penny and Brandon Burke as Alex.

CHARACTERS

MARGARET, a university history lecturer.
PETER, a professor of pure mathematics.
CONRAD, a television personality specialising in the environment.
JAQUIE, Conrad's wife, a former magazine journalist.
STEPHEN, a gloomy orthopaedic surgeon.
PENNY, his cheerful wife.
ALEX, a corporate lawyer.
VICKI, Alex's wife, a social climber.
JUSTIN, Conrad's son.

SETTING

The play is set in Crystal Inlet, a beachside settlement of weekenders where four couples escape from the pressures of city life.

ACT ONE

A wooden deck. Behind are the outlines of various houses. There are deck chairs and holiday furniture. The first house is MARGARET'S *a small tasteful cottage.*

MARGARET *moves forward. She looks down. She is looking at the ocean below. The methodical thud of the waves breaking can be heard. She is in her forties, attractive and trim.*

MARGARET: [*to audience*] Crystal Inlet is a small pretty bay two hours drive south of Sydney. People who can afford a holiday house make up most of the population. They go there on holidays and weekends to escape the monotony of their water views of Sydney Harbour. When my marriage split up . . .

[*She pauses, thinking*]

When my husband left me . . .

[*She pauses, thinking*]

When my husband discarded me six years ago for a woman fifteen years younger than I am, whose deficiencies are so gross I can't bear listing them, I kept the holiday shack down here at the Inlet and he kept the house in Sydney. I rent a house in Sydney which until recently I shared with my two daughters Micki and Tanya. They lived with me because nobody else can stand them, and the truth is, most of the time, neither can I, so I spend as much time down here as possible. Over the years a community of sorts has developed.

In fact, down here are my only real friends.

[*She pauses*]

Most of them appalling in their own special way, but then I'm scarcely perfect myself. I went to a psychotherapist for years. He said I was a very hostile person due to the fact that the world had fallen well short of my professional, personal and sexual expectations. He told me I had to start believing that life was essentially wonderful, but failed to come up with any significant evidence. He made about thirty five thousand dollars out of me so I suppose to him the world *was* pretty wonderful. I'm an academic. I teach history. I do not find it fulfilling.

* * *

The backdrop changes to another house. This one is even more modest than MARGARET'*s. A genuine old fibro cottage of the sort built in the fifties by retiring couples. History has lent its jerry-built irregularities great charm.* MARGARET *remains on stage and is joined by* PETER, *also in his forties. A very polite but not a timid man. An old- fashioned gentleman in the best sense.* PETER *sits in a deck chair in a hat to protect him against the sun. He is unaware of* MARGARET'S *presence. She indicates him. One of Bach's Brandenburg concertos plays softly in the background.*

[*to audience*] Peter isn't hostile. Peter is the least neurotic of my friends. Everybody likes him. His wife Claudia died recently. Breast cancer. Theirs was a truly happy marriage and at the time this particular story begins he was just starting to recover from deep and genuine grief. He and I work at the same University, and being neighbours down here at the Inlet, we often lunched together on campus to exchange gossip. When my husband left me Peter was compassionate and understanding, and when Claudia became ill I tried to repay the debt. We had become very good friends. Peter is a professor of pure mathematics who loves the beauty and power of mathematical abstractions. His papers are printed in international journals. He says nothing he's ever discovered has proved of use to anyone, which has given him an extremely high level of status in his chosen field.

[*Pause*]

A series of events happened last summer that constituted a kind of experiment into the nature of friendship. On a particular day, a few days after New Year, we all gathered for drinks on Peter's deck. Drinks on each other's decks was an old established tribal ritual.

[*Pause*]

On this particular day I had started the morning in a rare good mood. My two daughters who had threatened to come and stay decided they wouldn't. I suspect they were scared that during their week away from Sydney they'd miss a trend shift and on their return inadvertently turn up at the wrong nightclub.

[*She nods to the audience, 'Yes they are like that'.*]

But whatever the reason it was a blessed relief, because as soon as they get here they squeeze themselves into G-strings and strut around the beach and no one ever notices I'm alive. And they mess up the house faster than a pair of brain damaged pigs.

[*She shudders as she recalls the slovenliness of her daughters.*]

Then in the afternoon something happened that turned everything sour. As a result I arrived at Peter's deck in a mood that was unusually hostile --- even for me. For the first ten minutes or so I barely spoke.

[CONRAD WESSON, *a handsome, well preserved, genial man in his late fifties walks onto the deck with his wife* JAQUIE SWAN. JAQUIE *is pregnant. Obviously so. She is in her thirties and is an attractive and intelligent woman, but with a terse and sharply tough manner.* PETER *gets up to greet them and offer them drinks.* MARGARET *greets them but still remains the detached observer.*]

PETER: Conrad, Jaquie. Good to see you.

CONRAD: [*genially*] Glad to be here.

PETER: [*to* CONRAD] I really liked your show this week. I hadn't realised how much of the marine food chain starts in mangrove swamps.

CONRAD: [*nodding*] What the developers don't seem to realise is that if they bulldoze the mangroves to put up their hotels, the fish the tourists come to catch won't be there in ten years time. Greed, ignorance, apathy --- the deadly troika.

PETER: [*nodding*] It's depressing. What can I get you to drink?

CONRAD: White wine.

PETER: Jaquie?

JAQUIE: The same thanks Peter.

PETER: [*as he pours them*] Did you see Conrad's show this week Jaquie?

JAQUIE: [*shakes her head*] I turned it off. I can tolerate a fair degree of hypocrisy, but Conrad being humble . . . ? Foetus here gives me all the nausea I can handle.

[CONRAD *looks at* PETER *and shrugs, unconcerned. He seems to treat it as an oblique sign of* JAQUIE'S *affection.* PETER *hasn't quite got used to* JAQUIE'S *deadpan manner and feels a defence of* CONRAD *is needed.*]

PETER: I think Conrad comes across as very natural.

CONRAD: Thank you Peter.

JAQUIE: Millions are fooled. Who am I to complain?

MARGARET: [*to audience..*] Conrad Wesson and his third wife Jaquie Swan. Conrad's a biologist turned Media Conservationist. Turn on your television and there's Conrad taking us off to yet another Environmental Outrage. I'm not saying Conrad's not sincere. He is, but unlike many of us with similar feelings, he had managed to turn Environmental Concern into a nice little earner. You'll see his place a little later. Huge. Environmentally sensitive but *huge*. His wife Jaquie did lifestyle and interview pieces for upmarket magazines, and is as tough as chewed leather and smart as a snake.

[*Another couple comes onto the deck.* PENNY ARMSTRONG, *an attractive, smiling, optimistic woman in her mid forties, and her husband* STEPHEN ARMSTRONG, *a cadaverous-looking gloomy man of about the same age.* MARGARET, CONRAD *and* JAQUIE *exchange greetings.*]

PETER: Penny, Stephen. Good to see you. What can I get you to drink?

STEPHEN: Soda water.

PETER: Soda water. Sure. Penny?

PENNY: Wh ---

STEPHEN: [*interrupting*] I've given up alcohol. We're being poisoned by so many things we can't avoid it seems crazy to keep drinking something we can.

PENNY: White ---

STEPHEN: [*interrupting*] Do you know how much alcohol-related damage costs the economy? Eight billion dollars per annum.

PENNY: White wine thanks Peter.

[CONRAD *and* JAQUIE *move across as* PETER *pours the drinks.*]

PETER: [*lightening the mood; the good host*] Did you see Conrad's show on the mangrove swamps?

PENNY: I thought ---

STEPHEN: [*interrupting*] I don't have the time to watch television.

PENNY: I saw it Conrad. I thought ---

STEPHEN: In fact I can't even remember the last film I saw.

PENNY: *Pretty Woman.* Last Thursday. I saw it Conrad. I thought it was ---

STEPHEN: And what an appalling movie that was. Prostitute marries client and lives happily ever after.

PETER: [*coming to* PENNY'S *aid*] You liked Conrad's show?

STEPHEN: The world's got a massive AIDS epidemic on its hands and Hollywood's telling us prostitution is cute?

PENNY: [*to* PETER] Yes I did.

STEPHEN: It's easy to see why the Muslim religion is having such a resurgence all over the world. It's got the guts to say sleazy profiteers will *not* be allowed to make a fortune producing X-rated videos. Movie producers will *not* be allowed to make money out of films in which loveless sex, human dismemberment and death are the predominant images!

PENNY: Stephen, if you were living in a Muslim society you wouldn't have been allowed to watch your daughters play netball because you might glimpse female legs. Is that really the sort of society you want to live in?

CONRAD: Most of the legs I've seen in netball games would put you off sex for life.

STEPHEN: I didn't say I wanted to live in Muslim society. I just said there are certain things we could learn. Violence, rape and murder are escalating all over the western world.

PENNY: Stephen! We're on holiday. We're here to relax and enjoy ourselves. Just for a week or two I don't want to listen to unrelieved gloom!

MARGARET: [*to audience*] Penny Armstrong, one of the world's genuinely decent people, who had managed to preserve her buoyancy despite the fact that she was married to Stephen. She did two years of a law course, hated it because it was so adversarial, married Stephen who is toxically adversarial, raised two girls, went to art school and paints. She is exhibited occasionally in decent galleries and I think her work is fabulous, and keep buying it, but she hasn't got the push or confidence to sell herself. Stephen is an orthopaedic surgeon, and I can never quite rid myself of an image of him sawing human bones. Stephen is not a fun person to be with on social occasions. He makes Calvin seem like a starry-eyed soubrette.

[*Another couple arrives.* VICKI *and* ALEX CALABRESI. VICKI *is a woman in her early forties. Glamorously attractive. Her clothes are casual, tasteful and expensive.* ALEX *is swarthy and compact and exhibits a forceful, competitive and thrusting energy. They greet the guests.*]

PETER: Vicki, Alex. Great to see you --- what can I get you to drink?

ALEX: Bourbon on the rocks if you've got it.

PETER: I always keep some for you.

ALEX: I got into the hard liquor habit during our years in New York.

VICKI: Peter darling, if you put a large vodka and tonic into my right hand I will be eternally grateful. I have had an absolutely awful week.

PETER: What happened?

ALEX: [*sarcastically, sending his wife up*] Total disaster. A gallery opening, a charity ball, and two first nights.

VICKI: [*retaliating*] Alex, you *like* the social scene, I don't.

ALEX: So why is it *you* make *me* keep going?

VICKI: In the hope I'll meet someone genuinely interesting. Some hope. The same tired old faces, the same old jokes, the same pathetic knee jerk animation when the social photographer is nearby.

JAQUIE: You must have what it takes Vicki. I see you featured in the *Sun Herald* again this week.

VICKI: They didn't put me in *again*, did they? I can't *believe* it.

PENNY: Haven't you seen it?

JAQUIE: Of course she's seen it.

VICKI: Truly Jaquie, I rarely bother to look.

PENNY: You were standing with another woman.

VICKI: Wendy Weir, the film director's wife. [*Quickly correcting this giveaway that she has seen the photo.*] Most probably. I had a very interesting talk with the Weirs. Peter said he might come down to the Inlet, didn't he Alex?

ALEX: I never got near the guy. I don't have your skill with the elbows.

VICKI: Are you attempting some kind of pathetic public humiliation here Alex? You stood next to me while we spoke to Peter Weir.

ALEX: I stood next to you while two dozen people tried to shove us outa the way.

VICKI: [*terse, angry*] Alex, please don't do this. I talked to him for ten or fifteen minutes. We found out we have mutual friends, Sally and Robert, and I said the six of us should have a weekend down here. He said he would love to and we exchanged phone numbers!

[*Pause, as she glares at* ALEX]

If he comes we'll have drinks and you can all meet him.

[*A general murmur that that would be highly desirable but* ALEX *and* VICKI *continue to glare at each other.* PETER *moves between them to try and ease the tension.*]

PETER: I really like his movies.

[*They all nod and murmur that he is a wonderful film director.*]

MARGARET: [*to audience*] Vicki and Alex Calabresi. If there's a social ladder in sight, Vicki will climb it. Vicki's from established North Shore stock, but her mother ran off with her bridge tutor when Vicki was nine and Vicki needed to marry well to re-establish her social standing. [*She looks at Alex*] She failed. Alex's parents came here from Italy when Alex was four. His father made a fortune concreting driveways. His mother suffered acute social alienation and went mad. Alex pursued Vicki relentlessly and when his legal career started to take off she married him. He let it be known to the wedding guests that her dress cost three thousand dollars. She had already mentioned the figure five. The ensuing altercation established the future pattern of the marriage. They have a sweet son, Nicholas, whom I feel sorry for.

PENNY: How's Nicholas, Vicki?

ALEX: Got a good end of year report. We were proud of him.

VICKI: [*to* PENNY] He's sports crazy at the moment. I can't get two words out of him. All he does is grunt at me and leave those ghastly elastic pouches lying on the floor.

ALEX: Nicholas doesn't grunt! He's perfectly articulate.

PENNY: [*to* VICKI] My girls weren't great at communicating when they were fourteen either.

STEPHEN: [*staring at* PENNY *incredulously*] Our girls talked their heads off from the time they were two.

PENNY: [*to* VICKI, *ignoring him*] There's an age when they change from cute little things you can control, to gawky bad tempered little brats you can hardly bear to --- [*be with.*]

STEPHEN: [*interrupting*] Penny that's rubbish. They were always good kids and they were never any trouble.

PENNY: Perhaps I was with them more often than you.

STEPHEN: [*to* PENNY] What am I getting now? The full 'You've been a lousy father' number?

PENNY: [*to* STEPHEN] There *were* difficult times, whether you noticed them or not.

STEPHEN: The plain truth is our girls did *not* grunt at us when they were fourteen so why tell Vicki they did?

VICKI: [*to* STEPHEN] She was just trying to make me feel better. I know your girls weren't ever like Nicholas.

ALEX: Vicki, why are you dumping on Nicholas? He's a bloody good kid and he'd be even better if you gave him a bit more of your time and attention!

VICKI: [*angry*] Nicholas's perfect. Nicholas's wonderful. I'm just a lousy mother because I'm not thrilled at the sight of our mud covered son hurling himself at other mud covered sons. I am obviously a freak!

PETER: [*trying to change the subject, grasping at straws*] You think this Recession is long term Alex?

[*A good choice of topic by* PETER. *Only the economy could deflect* ALEX *from continuing his attack on* VICKI.]

ALEX: This is only the beginning mate. The economy's stuffed. I know dozens of guys --- unbelievable wealth --- financial stratosphere --- eighties superstars --- gone straight in with engine on afterburn ---

[*He makes a plummetting plane crash motion with his hand.*]

Merchant bankers driving taxis, stockbrokers selling hotdogs. I'll tell you something kiddos --- if your paycheck's not signed by the government it's Terror Time in Tinsel Town. Believe me.

VICKI: Close friends of ours, the Bassingtons, --- he was an *extremely* successful developer --- are taking their two sons out of Sydney Grammar and sending them to Vaucluse High. That's how bad it is.

ALEX: [*disputing this*] Who told you that. Roger or Laura?

VICKI: Roger.

ALEX: He's so fulla shit! He's still got seven to eight million in assets.

VICKI: He's taking those boys out of Grammar.

ALEX: Sure, and let every pissant in the city dump on him? [*Imitating an enemy*] 'Enjoying the opera Roger? Which school are your two lads going to?' He'd sooner shoot himself.

MARGARET: [*with an edge in her voice*] Alex, my kids went to State schools and so did Peter's and I don't think either of us got particularly suicidal.

ALEX: You're academics. You can plead legitimate poverty. For one of those guys to admit he couldn't afford to send his kids to a private school would be like admitting he had a half inch dick.

VICKI: Alex, why are you always so crude down here!

ALEX: I'm amongst friends for Christ sake! How long are you down here for Conrad?

CONRAD: Six weeks, thank God. The city's a bit of a hazard these days.

STEPHEN: [*nodding*] The Smog.

CONRAD: [*shakes head*] Too many people recognise me.

ALEX: [*sharply competitive*] It's a quality show but I wouldn't have thought it rated that high.

CONRAD: [*edgy, under challenge*] We're in the top ten.

ALEX: Great. [*Pseudo sympathy*] Chancy business though I guess. Ratings drop and you're dead meat.

CONRAD: Luckily, mine have been rising consistently for the last two years. [*Pseudo sympathy*] I was reading that law firms everywhere are putting off staff. Your firm OK?

ALEX: More work than we can handle. The guys I was advising

in the eighties I'm putting behind bars these days.

CONRAD: [*one upping* ALEX] Did I tell you I'm negotiating a deal for my show to go International? I'd be looking at ecological trouble spots all over the world.

JAQUIE: They want to make him the Clive James of the environment.

[*She raises her eyebrows as if to say 'what a joke.'*]

ALEX: They're pressuring me to become senior partner at Samuelson Bates. Lucrative as all hell but I'm into my forties and I'm not sure I want the stress. [*To* CONRAD] Going International will up *your* workload a lot won't it?

CONRAD: [*the precise thing that's been worrying* CONRAD] Three years of this deal and I'm set up for life.

ALEX: [*totally insincere*] Hope it comes off.

STEPHEN: If it wasn't for socialised medicine I would've been set up for life years ago.

PENNY: Stephen, we've got more than enough money.

STEPHEN: I went to a conference in the U.S. last year and every surgeon at my level is an extremely wealthy man. Private planes, mansions in France and Italy --- the lot.

PENNY: Stephen, we've got investment properties all over Australia.

ALEX: [*to* CONRAD] If you go international you'll be competing with some pretty polished performers.

CONRAD: [*on edge, definitely not laid back*] We think the market's ready for the no bullshit, laid back Australian style.

STEPHEN: [*to* CONRAD] I hope you start telling people how *really* serious things are. If we cut all CFC's tomorrow the hole in the Ozone layer will still get bigger for the next seventy years and there's no way we're going to cut carbon dioxide emissions in time to avert the greenhouse catastrophe.

CONRAD: I've got enough trust in the commonsense of humanity to believe that we'll take heed before it gets too late.

STEPHEN: [*gloomily and emphatically*] I haven't. Now the third world has started demanding everything we've got, the planet's as good as finished.

PENNY: Stephen ---

STEPHEN: In fifty years' time the Tasmanians who survived the melanomas will be drowning in tropical cyclones! The warning bells are ringing all over the globe. We are finally going to pay!

[VICKI *picks up a wine bottle, and pauses to speak before she pours.*]

VICKI: Why *does* the human species have this awful need to conspicuously consume?

[*She checks the wine label, seems satisfied that the quality is up to her standard and pours.*]

CONRAD: It's a form of male display, like the tailfeathers of a peacock.

VICKI: A mating strategy?

CONRAD: [*nodding*] To attract females. The more children you have, the more of your genes you leave behind and the unconscious agenda of all of us is the survival of our genes.

MARGARET: [*flinty*] The unconscious female agenda is to marry wealthy men?

CONRAD: [*nodding*] It gives their children, hence their genes, a better chance of survival. [*He beams, baiting her*] That's why successful older men like myself are in such demand.

JAQUIE: You all think he's joking don't you? By the time I found out he wasn't it was too late to get away.

MARGARET: Conrad, that's nonsense! Women are attracted to young men just like men are attracted to young women!

CONRAD: Younger men might look good but their genetic material is relatively unproven. They might turn out to be wimps who are never going to earn more than $50,000 per annum in their lives. Jaquie took one look at me and her subconscious computed 'Proven superior genes.'

JAQUIE: I'm obviously not in touch with my instincts because my conscious mind was saying 'Oh God, here comes that big mouth media greenie.'

[JAQUIE *gives* CONRAD *a mock smile and everybody laughs*

uneasily. CONRAD *seems unconcerned.*]

MARGARET: Has it ever occurred to you Conrad that you've constructed a world view that puts wealthy middle aged heterosexual males right at its centre?

CONRAD: [*genially*] Of course. And the best part is that it happens to be true.

[*There is a howl of disgusted protest from all the women, except* VICKI.]

VICKI: I find some of that plausible.

[MARGARET *stares at* JAQUIE *and* PENNY, *then at* VICKI.]

MARGARET: What particular part?

VICKI: That at a deep level a woman searches for the best genes for her child. Women tend to marry up into the social layer above them in every known society.

MARGARET: As every known society conspires to prevent women achieving in their own right, it might simply be that they want to live a slightly less awful life!

[VICKI *and* MARGARET *glare at each other. The tension is palpable.* MARGARET'*s hostility is a degree off boiling.* PETER *moves to try and defuse the situation.*]

PETER: What kind of host am I? Empty glasses everywhere. White wine Vicki? Penny? Margaret, tell me, what books should I be reading this summer?

MARGARET: Have you read A.S. Byatt's *Possession* yet?

[PETER *shakes his head shamefacedly.*]

ALEX: Who's A.S. Byatt?

VICKI: [*irritably*] She's Margaret Drabble's sister.

PETER: Is she?

MARGARET: Yes, but I don't think that fully defines the range of her achievements.

PETER: Is it good?

MARGARET: I think it's dazzling. It plays with the conventions of romance and yet manages itself to be an effective romance and it's also a very funny satire on academia.

STEPHEN: [*bitterly, to* PETER] I paid fifty dollars for a hardback copy of the Charles Dickens biography and the binding gave way as soon as I opened it.

VICKI: The review I read made it sound as if it was aimed at a fairly select audience Margaret.

STEPHEN: Incredible.

ALEX: I like a good strong story.

MARGARET: [*gritting her teeth*] In my opinion it's one of the most imaginative novels that's been written in the past twenty years.

STEPHEN: [*to* PETER] Can you believe that? You pay fifty dollars and a book literally falls apart?

MARGARET: There's this wonderful character called Maud Bailey ---

ALEX: You've got pretty rarefied tastes though Marg.

MARGARET: [*angry, a sudden full-on rage*] Not really. I simply attempt to be discriminating. If there *is* a point to life for me it's to explore the most challenging, the most imaginative and most thrilling work that the best minds of our time produce. I can't think what other possible purpose to life there could be! Yet when I come down here the only motives on display are making money, getting one's photo in the social pages, transmitting one's genetic endowment, or learning from the wisdom of the Ayatollah! I'm sorry, but it is utterly, utterly depressing!

[*They all stare at her.*]

[*to audience, as all but* PETER *leave*] The evening limped on. I guess by that stage I hadn't left anyone with all that much they could say.

* * *

Later. They are still both on PETER'S *deck. A scrabble set is on the table ready to play.*

PETER: Margaret.

MARGARET: They're appalling! If I was trying to make a case that material wealth equates with spiritual bankruptcy I'd know where to start looking.

PETER: Margaret, if you really don't like any of them wouldn't it be better to give these gatherings a miss?

MARGARET: Do you like them? Really?

PETER: Margaret, it's too easy to dismiss other people. We pit what they are, against what we *think* we are. We can always find excuses for our shortcomings but never theirs.

MARGARET: Peter, they're awful! Compare them with your other friends.

PETER: What other friends?

MARGARET: [*stares at him*] You and Claudia must have . . . had other friends?

PETER: Claudia and I and the boys used to spend every weekend down here.

[*Pause*]

I've got no illusions. Some of the things they've confessed to me when they've been drunk are hair raising, but I know them. They're tribe.

MARGARET: What things?

[*Pause*]

Have they confessed to you? When they're drunk?

PETER: I couldn't break their confidences. Appalling things, but in a way their fallibility makes them more endearing.

[*Pause*]

Life's been a bit of a nightmare for me lately. I really appreciate their company.

MARGARET: Of course. I'm sorry, I should have realised how important it is for you to have --- [*people around*]

PETER: It's not just Claudia.

[*Pause*]

I've lost everything I own.

MARGARET: [*frowning*] Lost everything?

PETER: I went guarantor for my brother Ray on the final bridging loan he needed to pull a big property development deal together in '88. A lot of money was being shifted out of the stockmarket and property was booming. I know in retrospect it was stupid but the bank assured me there was absolutely no risk --- it was just a legal formality, and I sort of felt I owed it to Ray ---

MARGARET: Because your parents had always made him feel that he was --- [*the dumb*]

PETER: [*nodding*] The dumb one of the family. Yeah, exactly. Then in '89 the property market collapsed, Ray went bankrupt and the bank was into me for everything I owned. The shack down here, the house in the city, my car, and probably half my income.

MARGARET: But if the bank told you there was no risk ---

PETER: Well exactly. I've just lost a court case I was sure I was going to win. That's why I didn't tell anybody.

MARGARET: But if the bank . . .

PETER: I've lodged an appeal, and my lawyers seem quite confident, but I owe them a hundred thousand or more already and unless I can come up with fifty thousand in cash I can't go on.

MARGARET: Can you mortgage your house?

PETER: Technically I don't own it any more. I don't own anything.

MARGARET: You must be out of your mind with worry?

PETER: [*nodding*] There's no way you can appreciate just how shattering poverty is until it's just about to happen to you. I haven't slept for weeks. I'm more worried about the boys than me. Richard'll be finishing his course in one more year, but Danny's still got three years to go.

MARGARET: Peter, this is awful.

PETER: I've gone back to my lawyers and asked if they'll keep going without the fifty thousand and they're considering it.

MARGARET: Is there a chance they will?

PETER: There's a chance.

MARGARET: If your lawyers turn you down you've got to tell the others. Conrad and Stephen and Alex are rolling in cash. They can lend you the fifty thousand.

PETER: I couldn't Margaret. If I lose the appeal they lose the lot.

MARGARET: If they're any sort of friends they should be willing

C Cruise
ChartMort
Chatham
Chelsea
Chew Corp

to risk it.

PETER: [*firmly*] You can't expect friends to pull you out of large scale financial strife.

MARGARET: Peter, friendship is more than just a herding ritual --- a little social gavotte we do to be entertained and amused. It involves the concept of help and support. If friendship had any reality, money would be *the* test.

PETER: I can't put them in that position.

MARGARET: Peter, all these years you've been the unofficial Father Confessor down here. For once in your life you need help.

PETER: You --- [*can't impose*]

MARGARET: If your lawyers say no, ask for it.

PETER: If I did I know they'd give it, but it's *my* problem.

MARGARET: Peter ---

PETER: I want you to promise you won't tell them.

[MARGARET *hesitates.*]

PETER: [*firmly*] Please. I mean it.

MARGARET: [*nodding*] All right.

PETER: I just couldn't bear to put them in that position.

MARGARET: All right!

[*Pause*]

I'm sorry I spoilt your drinks. I was in a foul mood when I arrived.

PETER: Something wrong?

MARGARET: I was stood up.

PETER: By who?

MARGARET: You've got enough problems without hearing mine.

PETER: Someone didn't turn up here?

MARGARET: [*nodding*] A friend of mine was supposed to take the train down here this afternoon --- I don't want to talk about it.

PETER: That er, chap you met at the conference?

MARGARET: No. After that disaster I swore I'd never go *near* another married man. Smug, overweight --- behaving as if he was doing me a huge favour. Some favour. Went home, blurted it all out to his wife, and she sent me a letter --- I wasn't ever going to tell anyone this --- asking me if I was proud of the fact that I had totally shattered her life. I wrote back that if she was the sort of person whose happiness depended on the fidelity of a near impotent, posturing, imbecilic, craven, tell tale sonk, then yes, I was very proud indeed.

[MARGARET *starts to distribute the scrabble pieces.*]

Vicki's having another affair, according to Jaquie.

PETER: She said she was coming up to talk to me.

MARGARET: You've got enough problems of your own.

PETER: I don't mind.

MARGARET: Why don't you tell her the truth for once?

PETER: Which is what?

MARGARET: Which is that ending up with Alex isn't a vicious quirk of fate, it's precisely what she deserves.

PETER: It can't be easy for her to be married to someone who's so contemptuous of her attempts to do something with her life.

MARGARET: Alex funds all the attempts and loses large sums of money every time. Her Boutique, her Travel Agency, her Restaurant.

PETER: That still doesn't excuse the way he treats her.

MARGARET: I'm not saying he's any better. Alex is naked self interest on legs. And as for Conrad ---

[*She shakes her head in disgust.*]

PETER: I like Conrad.

MARGARET: After the way he dumped poor Stephanie?

PETER: Yes, I must admit it was terrible timing.

MARGARET: [*disagrees*] Brilliant timing. She'd just finished redecorating. His third wife moved in and grabbed the lot. If I were Stephanie I'd bucket the bastard in the tabloids.

PETER: There's no doubt Conrad loves Jaquie. He can't wait for the new child.

MARGARET: Conrad counts his life's success as the number of genes he can spread to the next generation and Jaquie's his current incubator. And she was thirty six, in a tough profession, wanted kids and didn't want to be poor.

PETER: There's a touch of expediency in all relationships. I really like Penny.

MARGARET: So do I, but she should have the guts to leave Stephen. Who wants to be married to a man whose top of the range emotion is deep gloom?

PETER: [*conceding*] He can be quite intense.

MARGARET: Stephen is a black hole and Penny is being sucked in. Don't let Vicki come chattering up here with all her problems. You've got far bigger problems of your own.

PETER: I don't mind.

MARGARET: You're generous to a fault, which is why we all love you, but they're never going to learn anything if you just keep telling them that everything they do is fine.

PETER: I'm not *that* easy on them.

MARGARET: If, God forbid, this *is* going to be your last summer down here, the most enduring legacy you could leave the Inlet is a small dose of the truth.

PETER: I'm not that easy on them.

MARGARET: Peter, your idea of a severe reprimand is to stop smiling for ten seconds.

[PETER *stops smiling. He is clearly hurt.*]

MARGARET: Sorry. I wish I could be more generous about human frailty occasionally. Please let me tell them what's happened to you.

PETER: [*firmly, putting down his scrabble pieces*] No Margaret. No.

MARGARET: Peter, don't be such a --- [*She looks down at her scrabble pieces and begins picking them up and placing them rapidly on to the board*] Martyr. Twenty eight points.

[*She looks at him. He considers whether he should tell the others.*]

*   *   *

It is the next day. PETER *is sitting on his deck reading* Possession. *Schubert's* String Quintet in C Major *plays softly in the background.* VICKI *appears on his deck in a very attractive beach outfit.*

VICKI: Not beaching today?

PETER: I've never been much of a beach person.

VICKI: [*sitting down*] I came over to ask if you'd like to come to our place for drinks tonight.

PETER: That'd be great. Thanks.

VICKI: Was it just my imagination or was Margaret *particularly* appalling last night?

PETER: I think part of the explanation was that she was expecting a friend who didn't turn up.

VICKI: Can you blame them? She can be so overbearing. What I really find hard to take is her intellectual pretentiousness. Who'd *want* to read the books she reads except a small clique of overeducated pseudo intellectuals hell bent on self congratulation.

[PETER *discretely tries to hide his copy of* Possession.]

VICKI: What's that you're reading?

PETER: [*embarrassed*] *Possession.* Margaret lent it to me.

VICKI: Do you like it?

PETER: I've er, barely started.

VICKI: I've been worried about you Peter. You seem very pale. You don't look at all well. I know you'll never totally get over Claudia, but ---

PETER: [*hesitates*] It's not just Claudia.

VICKI: What's happened?

PETER: You came here to talk about *your* problems.

VICKI: No, please. Tell me.

PETER: No. Please. You first.

VICKI: [*hesitates*] Only, and I mean *only* if you tell me what's bothering you after I've said my piece.

PETER: It's a deal.

VICKI: Where do I start? You know the sort of trouble I've got myself into in the past.

PETER: Yes.

VICKI: On one level I'm tough as nails. On another a certain kind of man only has to look at me and I'm like a schoolgirl again.

PETER: You've fallen in love?

VICKI: [*nodding*] This makes all the others seem as if they were minor league. This one's a marriage breaker.

PETER: Some of the others went pretty close.

VICKI: They needn't've if Alex had've been able to keep some sense of perspective.

PETER: Alex has always seemed very tolerant.

VICKI: I'd hate to tell you the number of times that I've used makeup to disguise the black eyes and bruises. Six years at Sydney Grammar might have put on some surface gloss, but he's still a boy from the hills of Calabria.

PETER: Does he know about this one?

VICKI: I think he suspects.

PETER: So what are you going to do? Leave him?

VICKI: [*nodding*] I know what Alex is going to say . I've been swept off my feet because the guy is high profile. I don't give a damn about profile! It's the qualities that *made* the guy high profile that interest me.

PETER: How high profile?

VICKI: Very high profile.

PETER: Peter Weir?

VICKI: No, but he is in film. If I tell you, you won't tell anyone?

PETER: Of course not.

VICKI: Greg Hardboard.

[PETER *looks puzzled.* VICKI *looks annoyed. She expected the name to ring instant bells.*]

The producer.

[PETER *still looks puzzled.*]

Vera, The Desert Dwarfs.

[PETER *still looks puzzled.*]

Vera. Caused a sensation at Cannes last year.

PETER: The film everyone walked out of?

VICKI: The film that a handful of deeply conservative and moralistic critics walked out of. God, the Press back here! No wonder Greg wants to get out. Did they report what the *Le Monde* critic said? '*Vera* could be easily dismissed as an exploitation flick set in the flesh trade of the Philippines, but on another level it is a hymn of praise to human resilience.' Did any of our media report that? Did they report that *The Desert Dwarfs* is a sensational cult success in New York?

PETER: *The Desert Dwarfs*?

VICKI: It's an Eco - thriller. Chemical pollutant induced dwarf outcasts come in from the desert to replenish their gene pool by kidnapping tall girls. Greg would be the first to admit exploitative elements, but it was part of a deliberate strategy to pick up a development deal with a major American studio.

PETER: Has he?

VICKI: [*nodding*] He's just done a brilliant deal with Warner Brothers. For every one of their scripts he's allowed to do one of his. Do you know what his first one's going to be? *Middlemarch*.

PETER: The George Eliot novel?

VICKI: [*nodding*] A lot of people dismiss Greg because he left school at fifteen, but he's incredibly well read and has a *brilliant* mind. *Middlemarch* --- isn't that just so audacious. Getting Hollywood to finance the finest novel that's ever been written in the English language.

PETER: He's moving to L.A?

VICKI: [*nodding*] And he wants me there with him. Which is a real problem.

PETER: Nicholas?

VICKI: Nicholas.

PETER: How old is he now?

VICKI: Fourteen. If Greg was just wanting me over there as some Bimbo companion I wouldn't go. But he wants me right there working beside him. He says I've got the best intuitive grasp of script potential of anyone he's ever known.

For the first time in my life I've got a chance to create something lasting. To make a mark. But I *am* worried sick about Nicholas.

PETER: You'll leave him here?

VICKI: If I took him to L.A. Alex would be devastated. And if Alex was capable of being honest he'd admit there is a communication problem between Nicholas and I.

[*Pause*]

Sometimes it just doesn't happen between a parent and child and there's no sense pretending it has. I love him of course, but all that football and cricket --- all those male things --- that's something he shares with Alex. I know what people are going to say --- abandoning her child. Males do it all the time and nobody says a word.

[*Pause*]

What do you think about all this? Tell me honestly.

PETER: I don't really think I'm in a position to sit in judgement on .....

[PETER *looks at her and is about to complete something bland and forgiving when he remembers* MARGARET'*s exhortation to be honest. He steels himself and changes tack.*]

No, for once I'm going to be honest. Vicki, I'd be lying if I didn't say I was shocked. Nicholas is such a nice young kid.

VICKI: I love him. Don't get me wrong. I love him and I'm going to be commuting back every second month to see him. Peter, I've got to make something of my life and this could be my last chance.

PETER: And this guy, Greg --- *Middlemarch*?'

VICKI: O.K. that might never happen, but he'll try. Believe me he'll try.

[*Pause*]

If Greg *is* a disappointment, and can't lift his sights above exploitation movies, at least I'm over there working in the Industry. At least I've got a chance to be noticed and get my foot in the door.

PETER: [*sudden insight*] Greg is just a stepping stone?

VICKI: [*hotly defending herself*] No. Right at this moment Greg is someone I believe in very much. Peter, I've been waiting all my life for the sort of certainty I'm feeling now.

PETER: You've been certain before. The restaurant, the ---

VICKI: This time I'm *really* certain.

PETER: Look I know it can't be easy with Alex. I get embarrassed the number of times he attacks you in public ---

VICKI: That's nothing. That's Alex at his most charming, believe me.

PETER: I'm just very sorry for Nicholas.

VICKI: I'm devastated about Nicholas. But believe me what he's seeing of our marriage isn't doing him any good at all.

PETER: Vicki, it's your decision. I'm just an outsider looking in. You're the only one who knows your own heart, but I have to say that it sounds a little crazy to me.

VICKI: Peter, why are you suddenly being so judgemental? This is last chance time for me. I have very few options left in life.

PETER: Vicki, I'm sorry. I didn't mean to upset you, but I thought I should say what I honestly felt.

[VICKI *stares at him and gets up.*]

VICKI: [*as she goes*] You used to be someone who tried to understand.

[*She goes.* PETER *stands staring after her.*]

* * *

A few hours have passed. PETER *has progressed further into* Possession. *A Mozart quartet plays softly.* CONRAD *comes up onto the deck with an intense young man of twenty-four who is carrying a backpack.*

CONRAD: Peter. Hoped I'd find you here. This is my son, Justin.

[PETER *nods and shakes* JUSTIN'*s hand, but he is obviously a little bewildered. He can't recall* CONRAD *having a son of this age. Then it clicks.*]

PETER: Ah, yes. Justin. From your first marriage to er. . .

CONRAD: Barbara.

PETER: Barbara. [*Lying*] I've heard a lot about you from your father.

[JUSTIN *looks at* CONRAD *who tries to smile.*]

CONRAD: Right. He and Jaquie had a bit of a set to. I er, wondered if you had room to put him up for a day or two?

JUSTIN: [*intensely*] Conrad, I told you I'm not hanging around. I'm catching a train in the morning and I'm out of here.

CONRAD: Justin. I haven't seen you for years. Peter won't mind.

PETER: Of course not. That's fine.

[JUSTIN *looks at them both.*]

CONRAD: I was just walking around the headland and there he was. Sitting looking out at the ocean. I couldn't believe it. We haven't seen each other now for something like ---

JUSTIN: Eight years.

CONRAD: It can't be that long.

JUSTIN: Eight years.

CONRAD: [*to* PETER] We had a falling out which was just as much my fault as Justins.

JUSTIN: Why was it my fault?

CONRAD: [*exasperated*] O.K. Maybe it was more my fault. Let's not argue about that now. [*To* PETER] I've just got to go back and calm down Jaquie. I'll call back and see you both later.

[CONRAD *nods awkwardly at his son and leaves.* JUSTIN *and* PETER *stand there, both embarrassed.*]

PETER: Would you like a drink?

JUSTIN: No, I'm fine.

PETER: You decided to come and visit Conrad?

JUSTIN: No. I didn't even know this was where his holiday place was.

PETER: How come you were here?

JUSTIN: Look, I know you're a friend of his and I don't want to embarrass you, but I don't get on with him. I'll be gone in the morning.

PETER: Conrad seems to really want you to stay.

JUSTIN: Did you know he pissed off on Mum when I was only a year old?

PETER: No.

JUSTIN: All smiles on television. I wish they knew what he was *really* like.

[*Pause*]

I can't *believe* that new wife of his.

PETER: Actually she's a friend of mine too.

JUSTIN: I think she's a bitch.

[*There's an awkward pause.*]

PETER: Your father said you had a falling out eight years ago?

JUSTIN: [*upset*] Yeah. He didn't tell you why?

PETER: No.

JUSTIN: [*shakes head. Almost tears in eyes*] He told me he wasn't having me inside his house ever again. Eight years later --- same deal. Stay away.

PETER: He said you upset Jaquie.

JUSTIN: If she asks me stupid questions what am I supposed to do? Give her ten minute answers? I'm his son. Why do I have to go crawling around pretending to be nice?

PETER: Maybe she was just trying to be polite.

JUSTIN: I'm not stupid. I know when people are trying to be polite and she wasn't. She doesn't want to know about Conrad's other kids. She's got one of her own on the way.

PETER: It's natural for her to be preoccupied with the new baby.

JUSTIN: So where does that leave me? Absolutely nowhere. As usual.

PETER: Look, I know Conrad. He's basically a very warm person and it seems to me he wants you to stay and sort this thing out. What happened eight years ago?

JUSTIN: He took me out to this restaurant. Pretty crummy, but O.K. Said it was very special to him because it was the first real restaurant he ever ate in. I was actually pretty pleased. First time he'd ever bothered to take me out by myself. Do you know what it was about? To tell me I couldn't visit him any more because it was too distressing to his last wife Stephanie. Distressing? Bad luck for her. My whole life's been distressing. I wrote him a letter every week for years after, and got exactly two replies. Two!

PETER: That doesn't seem like Conrad.

JUSTIN: Two! Look I know I can't expect much. He's got four kids from his second marriage and I'm just one of three from his first. And now there's another one on the way. I guess I'd just like *some* consideration.

PETER: Absolutely.

JUSTIN: Do you know what he paid my Mum for my maintenance? Twenty dollars a week. The kids from his second marriage all went to private schools and this little brat's going to get the best of everything and he gave me exactly twenty dollars a week. I couldn't believe the house he's got down here. He must be absolutely loaded.

PETER: [*the conciliator*] Now you've had this chance meeting wouldn't it be worth trying to work things out?

JUSTIN: I don't want to work things out.

PETER: Wouldn't it be worth a try?

JUSTIN: What he did, he did. You can't undo the past.

PETER: I'm a father myself. I know what he's feeling. He obviously *has* acted callously if he only sent you two letters in eight years, and he needs you to forgive him. And I think somewhere inside you, you want to forgive him.

[JUSTIN *sits silently, trying to fight back tears.*]

You've got a lot of anger in you, and it's justified anger, but if you let it stay there it's going to block out a whole part of your life.

[JUSTIN *nods, still unable to speak.*]

[*patting him on the shoulder*] You can stay here. There's a spare room in there.

JUSTIN: Do you know someone down here called Margaret Connolly?

[PETER *stares at him.*]

PETER: Yes. She's a good friend.

JUSTIN: Does my Father know her?

PETER: Yes.

JUSTIN: [*heavy irony*] Great.

PETER: Why?

JUSTIN: That's why I'm down here. I came here to visit her.

PETER: Are you the person who was meant to be catching a train?

JUSTIN: [*surprised that he knows*] Yeah.

[*He notes the surprised look on* PETER'*s face.*]

Yeah. She's old enough to be my mother.

PETER: Sorry. When she told me I just assumed it was someone around er, my age.

JUSTIN: There's no law against me being friends with someone older.

PETER: No.

JUSTIN: I'm nearly twenty-five.

PETER: Right.

JUSTIN: All my other girlfriends have been younger than me and I have one relationship with an older woman and suddenly I'm a freak.

PETER: It doesn't worry me. Really.

[*Pause*]

JUSTIN: It worries everyone else. We walked into a restaurant holding hands the other night and everyone stopped and stared.

PETER: There is prejudice.

JUSTIN: I saw her waiting there at the station with crowds of other people around and I couldn't face it.

PETER: What did --- ?

JUSTIN: I hid. In the waiting room.

PETER: She was very upset. She thought you hadn't come.

JUSTIN: Were you ever involved with someone in their forties when you were only twenty-four?

PETER: No.

JUSTIN: Well it feels weird, and it feels even more weird when you find out she knows your Dad.

PETER: Didn't you tell her who your father was?

JUSTIN: We didn't spend much time talking.

[PETER *stares at him, absorbing the implication of hectic sexual activity.* MARGARET *steps onto the deck.*]

MARGARET: Hi. How are you finding *Possession* ---

[*She sees* JUSTIN *and stares at him.*]

PETER: You er, two know each other.

MARGARET: [*defensively*] So?

PETER: Justin is Conrad's son.

[MARGARET *stares at* JUSTIN].

JUSTIN: He saw me on the beach. I had no idea he had a place down here.

PETER: I'll put on the kettle.

[PETER *discretely disappears inside.*]

JUSTIN: I had a fight with his new wife. He brought me here.

MARGARET: Were you on the train?

JUSTIN: [*guilty*] Yes.

MARGARET: Didn't you see me?

JUSTIN: Yes.

MARGARET: So why didn't you ---

JUSTIN: You had this frown on your face. You looked as if you really didn't want me here. I stayed in the waiting room.

MARGARET: If I hadn't wanted you here, I wouldn't have asked.

JUSTIN: I thought you were probably bored with me. Everything I say must sound like a cliché to you.

MARGARET: Most of what I hear sounds like a cliché. Are you coming to my house or not?

[JUSTIN *hesitates. The palpable physical attraction between them competes with his embarrassment over her age and the fact that she knows his father.*]

JUSTIN: I should go and sort things out with my Dad first.

MARGARET: Why didn't you tell me Conrad was your father?

JUSTIN: You think I'd tell *anyone* that that grinning embarrassment on Channel 10 is my Father?

[*He retreats off the balcony.* MARGARET *looks at* JUSTIN'*s backpack which is still lying on the deck, picks it up, begins to move off, then stops, wondering if she should take it.* PETER *reappears with a milk carton in his hand about to ask* JUSTIN *if he takes milk in his tea.* MARGARET *quickly puts down the backpack.*]

MARGARET: Something bothering you?

PETER: No.

MARGARET: Conrad marries someone twenty years younger than he is and nobody bats an eyelid.

PETER: Exactly.

MARGARET: Well why are you looking so shocked?

PETER: I'm not. What you do is your own business.

MARGARET: He's very intelligent. He was doing arts honours and dropped out.

PETER: You don't have to justify anything.

MARGARET: I told myself I couldn't possibly bring him down here, then I thought 'Damn them', why not? So I rang him up and told him to take the train.

[*Pause*]

He's not the first one.

[PETER *attempts to be nonchalant.*]

[*guiltily*] I get bored and lonely and ---

PETER: You don't have to justify ---

MARGARET: I went to the State Gallery one Sunday --- and there was this young blonde guy with a backpack --- I reasoned that any young man who bothers to go to a gallery wouldn't be totally Neanderthal --- so I struck up a conversation with no other thought than maybe sharing a cup of coffee ---

PETER: What you do is your own business.

MARGARET: Conrad marries someone twenty years his junior and beams with pride and tells us he's obeying the immutable laws of the universe!

[*Pause*]

It's not that I *want* these --- liasons --- to be transient, but they all turn out to be tourists on their way somewhere else. Mostly Swedes. I usually get very fond of them, then off they go back to Sweden or Perth or wherever, and I cry. It's pathetic. [*Corrects herself*] Mostly I cry. Sometimes I breathe a sigh of relief. [*She imitates herself seeing one of the less notable off in the manner of a mother trying to be patient with a recalcitrant child.*] You've got your ticket, you've got your backpack. Goodbye Sven.

[*Pause*]

I should stop it shouldn't I?

PETER: It's entirely up to you.

MARGARET: [*suddenly angry*] Peter, be *honest*! Of course I should stop it. It's dangerous and self destructive.

[*Pause*]

I make them wear condoms, but I can't protect myself if one of them turns out to be a psychopath, can I?

PETER: OK, then stop.

MARGARET: [*still angry*] The world of mathematics might be beautifully logical, but *we* aren't. I have tried to stop, but suddenly I find myself stalking the Gallery again, lying to myself that this time it's for the art, smiling at that handsome blonde chap with the red backpack, and trying to pretend that my rising levels of excitement are due to that exquisite new Chinese section on the second level. I want to stop but I can't!

PETER: How er many of these er ---

MARGARET: Three or four.

[*Pause*]

Six or seven.

PETER: Why not look for someone permanent? Remarry?

MARGARET: [*sarcastically*] Peter, have you read the statistics? If you're a woman, turned forty and have a University degree, let alone a doctorate, the chances of you getting re-married are considerably less than becoming a female astronaut, and given what happens to them I'm not tempted to take that up as an alternative!

PETER: I'm sure there'd be a lot of men who'd ---

MARGARET: Since Max walked out on me the best offer I'd had

INDUSTRIAL SHARE LIST
MINING AND OIL

was from a lesbian in Sociology called Naomi. And if she had've been just a tiny bit more personable I might have given it a try!

[MARGARET *stands there looking at* PETER.]

* * *

STEPHEN *stands on his balcony staring at the deck below. The house behind the deck is much bigger than* PETER'*s or* MARGARET'*s. It has wooden beams and timber in a style that would have been modern when it was built twenty years before. He has a screwdriver in his hand.* PENNY *comes out onto the deck carrying a freshly baked quiche in her hands. He looks up at her.*

STEPHEN: [*indicating the balcony*] Dry rot. Right through the bearers.

PENNY: Is it serious?

STEPHEN: I just told you. It's right through the bearers. We'll have to cancel Wednesday's drinks.

[*She stares at him.*]

A dozen people up here and the whole deck could collapse.

[PENNY *stamps on the deck.*]

Don't do that! It's a five metre drop. [*Indicating the quiche*] Who's that for? Peter again?

PENNY: It's just a way of letting him know we care. It'll be years till he gets over Claudia. Do you really want me to cancel the drinks?

STEPHEN: I just told you. The whole deck's about to collapse.

PENNY: Should we call in someone to look at it?

STEPHEN: Who? That crook down the road?

PENNY: We'll have to do something eventually.

STEPHEN: [*irritated*] I'll get it fixed? OK? But I'm not getting that crook down the road.

PENNY: [*quietly*] Have you got any idea when ---?

STEPHEN: No! Absolutely none! Just cancel the drinks and I'll get onto it as soon as I can, OK?

PENNY: Is there something you want to talk about?

STEPHEN: Talk about?

PENNY: I thought there might be. You haven't spoken to me since yesterday.

STEPHEN: Maybe there's a reason for that.

PENNY: That's why I thought we should perhaps talk about it?

STEPHEN: [*the floodgates of resentment lifted*] I don't enjoy being humiliated in front of our friends!

PENNY: I'm sorry. I really love our daughters and I didn't mean to imply we had any great problems with them. I was just trying to make Vicki feel a bit easier about Nicholas.

STEPHEN: By telling everyone our girls grunted?

PENNY: [*calmly patient*] By letting her know that *all* fourteen year olds are a little bit difficult.

STEPHEN: Name me one time when one of our girls was difficult at the age of fourteen. One time!

[PENNY *searches frantically through her mind.*]

STEPHEN: You can't, can you?

PENNY: [*keeping calm*] I can't right now, but I know there were.

STEPHEN: Why did you let everyone know about the property we own?

PENNY: Because we do.

STEPHEN: That's private and confidential. That's between you and me and no one else!

PENNY: What does it matter? Most of them are well off too.

STEPHEN: Not as well off as we are. They think they are but they're nowhere near it.

PENNY: What harm is it if they know?

STEPHEN: Because when someone like Vicki gets a piece of information like that it's all over Sydney!

PENNY: Stephen ---

STEPHEN: Have you been reading about all the kidnapping and extortion stuff lately?

PENNY: Stephen our daughters are grown up ---

STEPHEN: I just don't want *anyone* to know how wealthy we are.

Anyone! OK? And I really, really resented the way you painted me as a fanatical Muslim!

PENNY: Well you did say ---

STEPHEN: I said I can understand why the Muslims are having a resurgence --- I didn't say I thought we should embrace their religion!

PENNY: I thought you were being just a bit too --- strident.

STEPHEN: You've been shocked by the sex and violence in the media yourself, but when someone's got the guts to speak up about it all you can do is ridicule!

PENNY: I thought you were ---

STEPHEN: [*interrupting*] I've worked like a slave for years and years so I could give you and the girls a decent life, and when you attack me like that in public I wonder what the hell it's all been for!

PENNY: Stephen ---

STEPHEN: [*interrupting*] You set me up beautifully for that bitch Margaret, didn't you? 'Learning from the wisdom of the Ayatollah.'

PENNY: She was sounding off at everyone.

STEPHEN: Me in particular. She's had me in her sights ever since I said that Salman Rushdie must have known what he was letting himself in for. I really can't *stand* her or any of the rest of them.

PENNY: Stephen, they're our friends!

STEPHEN: [*as he paces gingerly round the rotting deck, testing the strength of the bearers*] Conrad making a fortune out of watered down environmental pap, Jaquie producing more of his bloody kids when there are five billion of us around already, Alex working as a hired gun for any crook who can pay the fee and Vicki, the North Shore nympho. Why does anyone bother! I'm not sorry the deck has gone rotten. I don't want any of them up here in any case.

[*He turns and walks inside.*]

PENNY: [*to herself*] Why not? You could get rid of us all in one hit.

STEPHEN: What?

PENNY: [*to herself*] And if you were around we'd be happy to go.

STEPHEN: What?

PENNY: I said I am going to deliver this quiche.

STEPHEN: [*from inside*] Walk. Don't take the car. The oil warning light's still showing.

* * *

PENNY *appears on* PETER'*s balcony. She is warm and sunny, apparently without a care in the world. She is carrying a quiche in her hands.* PETER *is still reading. Music plays softly. It is the* Queen of the Night *aria from Mozart's* The Magic Flute. *He looks up when he sees her. He tries hard to disguise it but it's obvious he finds her very attractive.*

PENNY: Hi, just came by to see if you could use one of these.

PETER: Penny, you shouldn't keep doing this.

PENNY: I cooked a batch. It's no trouble.

PETER: That's very kind.

[*He puts the book down and takes the quiche.* PENNY *looks at the backpack lying on the deck.*]

PENNY: Visitors?

PETER: Conrad's lad from his first marriage.

PENNY: Why isn't he staying --- [*sudden insight*] Jaquie?

PETER: [*simultaneously*] Jaquie.

[*They laugh warmly*]

PENNY: [*looking at book*] *Possession*?

PETER: Margaret dropped it in.

PENNY: How is it?

PETER: Post-modern novels are a bit of a problem for me. I haven't read enough to know which literary styles are being parodied.

PENNY: What sort of books do you normally read?

PETER: Anything in the general area of complex number theory, and Mystery, Private Eye and Crime.

PENNY: Elmore Leonard?

PETER: [*kindred soul*] Wonderful. *Freaky Deaky*? *Glitz*?

PENNY: [*nodding*] I love his stuff. *Killshot*?

PETER: [*nodding*] *Get Shorty*?

PENNY: *Get Shorty*.

[*They laugh and exclaim in the pleasurable recollection.*]

PETER: Isn't it heaven to pick up a book and know the author's bothered to think up a *plot*?

PENNY: I love his characters. They're so sleazy and amoral.

PETER: I've known you all these years and had no idea you were into Crime.

[*They laugh again.*]

PENNY: What exactly are complex numbers?

PETER: Numbers that don't strictly exist, but if they did they'd be very interesting.

PENNY: [*smiling, then sober*] We've had to cancel our drinks on the deck this Wednesday. Sorry.

PETER: Oh. So am I.

PENNY: Stephen's discovered some dry rot in the planking and he's got the idea that the whole deck might collapse if we have too many up there, so I've got to wait till he gets it checked.

PETER: There'd need to be a lot of dry rot. You've got bearers 25 cms thick.

PENNY: [*sighs*] Well you know how he is.

[PETER *nods.* PENNY *debates whether she'll say something.*]

Peter, Stephen's very upset about last night up here. He thinks I was undercutting him. Did you think I was?

PETER: Not at all ---

[PETER, *about to deliver one of his bland reassurances, remembers* MARGARET'*s accusation that he is too soft*]

Penny, for once I'm going to tell the truth. Yes, you were, but if you want my frank opinion he deserved everything he

INDUSTRIAL SHARE LIST
MINING AND OIL

got and more.

[PENNY *looks at him. Surprised at his frankness.*]

The thing I've wondered about all these years is how come someone as optimistic and positive as you got together with him?

PENNY: I think I had too much unfocussed missionary zeal. I knew he had a dark side, but I thought I could change him.

[*Pause*]

He saw through all the ways we were being manipulated --- by politicians, advertising, the media. I guess I confused intelligence with paranoia.

[*Pause*]

Have I told you the saga of the video recorder?

[PETER *shakes his head.* PENNY *starts to smile despite herself. The incident seems so bizarre.*]

Our VCR broke down so Stephen decided to get a new one. I said get a simple one, but he wanted state of the art, so we got state of the art. All we ever use it for is to watch videos but because this machine can do one hundred and seventeen functions, Stephen *had* to conquer them all. Which is fine, except no one with an IQ less than two hundred and twenty has ever been able to decipher the manual. After a week of total rage, in which nobody dared mention the word 'Japan', he took it back, but because Stephen's attitude to the world is that everyone's going to give him a hard time, of course everyone does. He walked into the place bellowing that any shop that stocked this model should be hauled up before the consumer complaints tribunal, and demanded an exchange.

PETER: They refused?

PENNY: They told him to get stuffed.

[*Pause*]

We're six weeks into litigation and I'm beginning to feel I'm never going to see a video again in my life.

[PETER *is by now laughing out loud. So is* PENNY, *more out of relief than anything.*]

It's not really funny is it?

PETER: Why is he like that?

PENNY: [*shrugging*] His mother said he came out angry and stayed that way. I keep thinking maybe I'm exaggerating the problem. Maybe other people don't think he's so bad.

PETER: They do.

PENNY: It has been harder for me since the girls moved out. At least we could laugh about him together.

PETER: Why do you .. ? Have you ever .. ?

PENNY: Thought of leaving him? I've done it. Twice. And he begs me to come back. Underneath he's very vulnerable.

PETER: Yes but ---

PENNY: And really quite decent. He just doesn't realise *how* negative he is.

PETER: [*glint in his eyes*] It's about time someone told him.

[JUSTIN *comes storming onstage. He is about to say something when he notices* PENNY. PENNY *has already noticed him and is more than impressed.*]

JUSTIN: Hi.

PETER: Justin, this is Penny. Penny, this is ---

PENNY: Conrad's son.

[*She indicates the backpack.*]

Peter explained.

[JUSTIN *nods but is preoccupied with his father.*]

PETER: You spoke to your Father?

[JUSTIN *nods.*]

PETER: Not good?

JUSTIN: Hopeless. He can't even begin to understand what it's been like for me. And he doesn't even want to try.

PETER: I'm sorry.

JUSTIN: [*to* PETER] I can't *believe* he's behaving like this. I can't believe he doesn't realise what impact his walking out had on my life!

PETER: These things aren't resolved in a day.

JUSTIN: [*to* PENNY] You're er, staying here with --- [PETER]?

PETER: [*quickly*] No Penny is married to Stephen. They've got a house over there.

[*He points.*]

JUSTIN: [*to* PENNY] I guess you know Conrad too?

PENNY: Yes, . . . I think he's a bit tense . . . Jaquie being pregnant . . . Jaquie being Jaquie . . .

JUSTIN: I hope they have brilliant sex. They're not getting anything else out of that relationship.

[PENNY *looks at* PETER. MARGARET *comes onstage.* PENNY *is nearest to* MARGARET.]

PENNY: Hi. Oh Margaret. This is Justin, Conrad's son from his first, very first, marriage.

PETER: Margaret and Justin have met.

MARGARET: [*nodding*] Hello Justin.

PENNY: Justin's come here to sort things out with Conrad, but it doesn't seem to be working out.

JUSTIN: [*embarrassed, looking at* MARGARET] Actually I came here to see a friend.

PENNY: Male or female?

JUSTIN: Female.

PENNY: [*to* MARGARET, *conspiratorially*] Lucky friend.

JUSTIN: Sorry?

PENNY: Sorry. I said lucky friend. If I wasn't married to one of the world's most charming men, and I was twenty years younger I'd be trying to supplant her.

[*Pause*]

I can't believe I just said that. I can't believe you're Conrad's son. Your mother must have been *very* beautiful. Penny stop this. Justin, I'm sorry. I'm either suffering pre-menopausal hysteria or you are a very attractive young man. Say something Margaret.

MARGARET: [*coldly*] Why twenty years younger?

PENNY: Sorry.

MARGARET: Why would a woman need to be twenty years younger to contemplate a relationship with Justin?

PENNY: [*thinking*] No reason. No reason at all.

MARGARET: [*to* JUSTIN] Justin's involved with someone older than him right now, aren't you Justin?

close to 71,000.
creating
regional
INDUSTRIAL SHARE LIST
Company
Last sale
Closing
Year's range of sales
Company
Last Sales
sold 100s
range of sales
A Min Fnd
A.O.V Min
ACM Gold
ADEX ctg
ADEX ctg
AOG
Aberfoyle

JUSTIN: [*edgy*] That's right.

PENNY: [*transfixed*] Really.

MARGARET: And is there anything embarrassing or unsatisfactory because of that?

JUSTIN: No.

PENNY: In fact, come to think of it I read somewhere that young men appreciate the fact that older women *know* so much more. Not just sexually, but in general.

JUSTIN: [*nodding*] This woman's got me enthused about literature again. [*Looks at* MARGARET] And she's really, really sexy.

PETER: Isn't this all a little bit embarrassing?

MARGARET: No!

PENNY: How did you get to er, meet?

JUSTIN: In the State gallery.

PENNY: Really. I haven't been for a while. People accept a younger man older woman relationship?

JUSTIN: It hasn't been going long.

PENNY: I would have thought there was still prejudice.

JUSTIN: A bit, [*He looks at* MARGARET *guiltily*] but apart from that it's been great.

MARGARET: [*sharply*] So why aren't you there? At this woman's place?

PENNY: He's trying to sort things out with his father. Jaquie's being appalling, as usual.

JUSTIN: My father's being appalling. All I'm asking is the right to be treated like his son.

PETER: [*eager to get him away from* PENNY] Why don't you give it one more try?

JUSTIN: You think?

PENNY: Absolutely. If I was a father I'd be *proud* to have a son like you. Proud.

PETER: Bring up the letters. Tell him how hurt you were to only get two replies.

JUSTIN: The letters --- yes of course!

PENNY: I'll come with you. I'm going that way. I'm going for a walk in the National Park. If you want to cool down before you see him, it's a beautiful walk.

JUSTIN: No, I'll catch him now. I'd forgotten about the letters.

[*He nods goodbye to* PETER, *then* MARGARET *and goes.*]

PENNY: I have to go for a walk. Stephen's still fuming about the fact I let slip that he's rich. He hates anyone to know he's rich.

[PENNY *catches sight of* JUSTIN. *She calls out after him as she leaves.*]

Justin. I'll go with you as far as Conrads.

[MARGARET *watches her go and turns to* PETER.]

MARGARET: Pre-menopausal hysteria? She's acting like she hasn't had sex for six years.

PETER: Which could --- [*well be true*].

MARGARET: [*nodding*] Well be true. If Stephen doesn't do something soon she'll leave him

PETER: I still think she cares about him.

MARGARET: Like you care about a nail in your shoe. Peter, you're a hopeless romantic. Just because *you* had a perfect marriage ---

PETER: It wasn't perfect.

MARGARET: [*conceding*] I did hear you once have a disagreement about whether to switch the heater on, but for the most part it was one long irritating saga of mutual bliss. [*Sudden thought*] Penny would be perfect for *you*!

PETER: [*shocked*] Penny?

MARGARET: For certain women a quiche is the female equivalent of a dozen red roses.

PETER: Margaret!

MARGARET: Have you ever had sexy thoughts about her?

PETER: [*lying*] No. Never. Margaret, there's no way I'd ever run off with another man's wife! Besides, what have I got to offer? Invitation to poverty.

MARGARET: Peter, you don't have to be poor. If your lawyers insist on their fifty thousand, ask your friends. They're all rich. You heard Penny ---

PETER: Margaret, please --- [*let's not go into*]

MARGARET: If the Bank grabs half your income you'll have to live in some terrible little one bedroomed ---

PETER: I know. Don't remind me.

MARGARET: You've got to let me tell them.

PETER: [*firmly*] No.

MARGARET: You've *got* to go to court and appeal.

PETER: My father used to say you can ask a friend for anything except money, and I think ---

MARGARET: That's stupid.

PETER: And I think he was right.

MARGARET: Why?

PETER: Because you're as good as telling them that if they don't pay up they're no longer your friend. You're coercing them. You're not giving them any choice. I couldn't bear to do that.

[MARGARET *accepts that this is his final word and goes to leave, looking down at the backpack.*]

MARGARET: Everytime I come up on your deck that thing's sitting there staring at me!

PETER: Take it.

MARGARET: [*is about to then changes her mind*] No. He can bring it. If he ever gets round to wanting to come.

PETER: He said really nice things about you.

MARGARET: And about the difficulties. We were in a restaurant the other night and one person looked at us and he nearly froze. Have you ever seen Penny like that before? She and Stephen must be on their last legs.

PETER: [*nodding*] That's what I'm worried about. I'm going up to talk to Stephen now.

MARGARET: Talk to him?

PETER: Yes. I'm taking your advice. If it *is* going to be my last summer here, I owe it to everyone to be honest.

[MARGARET *stares at him.* PETER *moves off.* MARGARET *hesitates then does pick up the backpack and takes it.*]

* * *

PETER *walks up onto* STEPHEN *and* PENNY'*s deck.* STEPHEN *is sitting on a deckchair in a depressive trance staring straight ahead with a screwdriver in his hand and a worried frown on his face.*

PETER: Hello there.

STEPHEN: Penny's not here. She's out walking. She walks a lot. In the National Park.

PETER: Actually I came to see you.

[STEPHEN *stares at him.*]

Penny and I have been talking about some problems you've been having ---

STEPHEN: [*nodding*] Dry rot. Right through the bearers. The leaves get caught in the gaps and stay damp. The architect should have realised. Alex thinks I might be able to sue him. It's only been built twenty years.

PETER: She mentioned the dry rot but it was actually --- [*something else I wanted*]

STEPHEN: The cracks should have been either further apart or the planks should have been butted close.

PETER: You're both my --- [*very good friends*]

STEPHEN: You work for years to get something decent and it all falls apart.

[PETER *looks at him, then takes the screwdriver out of his hand, walks onto the deck and probes the extent of the dry rot.*]

PETER: It's only a centimetre deep. You've got another twenty four to take the load.

[STEPHEN *looks at him. Almost uncomprehending.*]

Eventually someone will have to replace the joists, but I think these ones will see you out.

[STEPHEN *stares at him.*]

Penny and I have discussed some problems she felt you were both having.

[STEPHEN *stares at him.*]

STEPHEN: I thought she must have talked to someone. She said she's not going to listen to any more of my gloom.

PETER: You have certain views about things and so does she ---

STEPHEN: [*interrupting*] Isn't that absolutely normal?

PETER: Stephen, this deck was never going to collapse.

STEPHEN: OK, so occasionally I worry too much. Is that a crime?

PETER: Stephen ---

STEPHEN: Is that any reason to tell my wife she's got a perfect right to ignore me?

PETER: Stephen, the reason I'm telling you all this ---

STEPHEN: What sort of friend are you?

PETER: --- is that if you don't do something, you might lose her for good.

STEPHEN: [*onset of panic*] She's said she's going?

PETER: No, she hasn't. Stephen ---

STEPHEN: That's it, isn't it?

PETER: I'm sure there's still a lot of love between you if ---

STEPHEN: She said it didn't she. She's going to leave?

PETER: No, she didn't.

STEPHEN: I'd rather know.

PETER: She didn't. Truly.

STEPHEN: I've given that woman everything she ever wanted ---

PETER: She didn't say she was leaving ---

STEPHEN: Worked like a dog.

PETER: She just thinks ---

STEPHEN: Thinks what?

PETER: That you don't quite realise how negative you can be.

STEPHEN: Some people would call it realistic! Some people would call it honest! Some people would be pleased I don't let myself get pushed around! If it annoys her so much why doesn't she let me know!

PETER: Stephen, she does. Time and time again. You've both got to the stage where you don't *hear* each other any more.

STEPHEN: I know what you all think. She's the sweetie and I'm the rat! Bakes you quiches and you think butter wouldn't melt in her mouth! Well it's not that simple. Headache every night. 'Can't we just cuddle. Can't we just be friends?' [*Darkly*] You don't know the half of it.

PETER: I'm sure there are --- [*two sides to*]

STEPHEN: There's no need for her to walk out. We can fix it. She's the most important thing in my life.

PETER: Have you *told* her that lately?

STEPHEN: You don't need to say things over and over! Certain things are understood.

[STEPHEN *looks at him defiantly, turns and goes inside.* PETER *turns and goes.*]

* * *

MARGARET'*s deck. A thunderously anguished passage of Shostakovich's tenth symphony is playing.* MARGARET *is pouring water into a bowl. She looks up as* PETER *steps onto her deck, and ducks inside to turn down the music.*

MARGARET: I always feel better if the music is marginally more tortured than I am. [*Indicating the bowl*] For the Lorikeets. Do they come to your deck?

PETER: [*nodding*] Rainbows and Greens. I cheat. I put sugar in a bowl and they come in flocks.

MARGARET: [*rebuke*] Sugar makes their eggshells crack. Still no sign of Justin.

PETER: He must be still sorting things out with his father.

MARGARET: [*irritated*] What exactly is he sorting out?

PETER: He needs to feel Conrad values him. He was left when he was one year old.

MARGARET: One year of Conrad would surely be less emotionally damaging than twenty four.

PETER: I was just on my way to Alex and Vicki's drinks. Are you coming?

MARGARET: Can't we think of an excuse?

PETER: [*shaking his head*] Alex is unveiling his new Beefeater barbeque.

MARGARET: I faked an envy attack over his new Mercedes, but I *can't* pretend I'm desperate for a Beefeater barbeque. Please let's not go.

PETER: You enjoy the drinks ritual more than anyone.

MARGARET: Are you joking?

PETER: Where else could you feel superior so often and so easily?

MARGARET: [*nodding*] I knew there had to be some reason I keep going. Is everyone coming?

PETER: I don't think Stephen will be there.

MARGARET: He didn't react well?

PETER: [*shakes head*] A sort of frenzied depression.

[*Pause*]

You were right. I've started telling everyone what I really think. I should have done it years ago.

MARGARET: Who have you been telling?

PETER: Stephen, Vicki, Penny ... and there's something I want to say to you.

[MARGARET *stares at him, bemused.*]

MARGARET: Go ahead.

PETER: Forget Justin. It's not just the age thing. He's obviously the answer to just about every woman's prayers, but he's not a long term answer for you.

MARGARET: I wasn't planning to marry him.

PETER: Losing Claudia was the worst thing that's ever going to happen to me. It's not *easy* to find someone who's right for you but it's worth the effort.

MARGARET: [*coolly*] Finished?

PETER: No, I haven't. You've got to stop ---

MARGARET: What?

PETER: Picking up these boys!

MARGARET: [*irritated*] Peter, I'm in a better position to judge what I need for my life than you!

PETER: I had to tell you how I honestly felt.

MARGARET: I've heard how you honestly felt. Now I'll tell you how I feel. I feel like I want to take Justin to bed and screw him for the rest of the week. Do you think men are the only ones who get those sort of urges? Do you think men are the only ones entitled to feel like that? If you see him before I do will you tell him to sort things out with his stupid father and come and see me! Soon!

[PETER *stands there shocked at her outburst. He turns his back on her. Almost immediately she feels remorseful. After a pause. He turns around again.*]

MARGARET: Sorry.

PETER: You were the one who told me to tell the truth.

MARGARET: Sorry.

[*Pause*]

Let's go and gasp at Alex's Beefeater.

[MARGARET *goes and links arms with him.* PETER *relaxes. They are friends again. They move off.* MARGARET *comes downstage.*][*To audience*] The last thing anyone wants to hear is usually the truth. If Peter had known what was in store for him up on Vicki and Alex's deck he might've found an excuse not to go after all. You'll see all that --- after interval.

ACT TWO

VICKI *and* ALEX*'s house. Large, expensive and ultra modern. Ash coloured bleached timbers, blue and green paintwork and skylights. The message - money and plenty of it. The music is the Chicago tune* It's Hard to Say I'm Sorry. VICKI, ALEX, CONRAD *and* JAQUIE *are there. There is muted and sporadic conversation going on between them, but an air of obvious tension pervades the atmosphere. It's as if they are waiting for the arrival of someone. In fact they are:* PETER. *He arrives with* MARGARET *and the conversation temporarily halts. Perfunctory greetings are exchanged. There's a total lapse in the conversation.* PETER *feels uneasy. Eyes are on him. He and* MARGARET *move to* ALEX*'s new barbeque to try and politely fake envy.*

PETER: [*to* ALEX] That's a very impressive Beefeater Alex.

ALEX: [*coldly*] Yeah.

PETER: How much did it cost?

ALEX: Heaps.

VICKI: Conrad, where's that young lad of yours? I thought you were probably going to bring him?

[CONRAD *looks at* JAQUIE. JUSTIN *is obviously still a huge source of tension.*]

CONRAD: No, he er, went down the beach.

VICKI: Very nice looking young boy. I thought to myself if I was twenty years younger --- [*She raises her eyes*] Well.

[MARGARET *is annoyed but keeps her tongue in check.*]

PETER: [*to* CONRAD] Did you er, sort something out --- [*with him?*]

CONRAD: [*emphatically*] No!

[MARGARET *raises her eyes to the sky. When in the hell will* JUSTIN *sort the damn thing out? There is another silence.* CONRAD *inclines his head at* JAQUIE, *indicating that she should get the women inside.*]

JAQUIE: [*looking inside the glass front*] You've had everything re-covered Vicki?

VICKI: It was just getting a tad too tatty in there.

JAQUIE: Can we take a look?

VICKI: Of course. You were going to have yours done weren't you Margaret?

[MARGARET *follows them out of duty. There is another awkward silence in which* PETER *feels increasingly uncomfortable.* CONRAD *advances on* PETER.]

CONRAD: Thanks a million.

PETER: Sorry?

CONRAD: Jaquie and I have just had one of the worst days of our life.

PETER: Justin?

CONRAD: [*nodding*] Screamed at me non stop.

PETER: He seems pretty upset too.

CONRAD: He said that in your opinion I'd treated him like shit!

PETER: That's not true.

CONRAD: What did you say?

PETER: I said that it seemed odd you hadn't replied to his letters.

CONRAD: Letters! [*Angrily*] Did he tell you what was *in* the letters?

PETER: No.

CONRAD: Did he tell you what happened eight years ago.

PETER: He said you flew down and met him in a restaurant.

CONRAD: I couldn't have him come and visit me in Sydney any

more, because he was paying out Stephanie and the kids in an extremely aggressive way and wrecking what was left of my second marriage --- little acts like picking up the bill in a restaurant and saying in a very loud voice, 'This is more than Mum has for food for a week,' --- so I decided I'd go down to Melbourne and tell him that instead of him coming up, I'd go down there every month and we'd have lunch and talk. I took him to a little restaurant that really meant a lot to me. Pelligrinis. The first Italian restaurant I ever went to at the age of seventeen, and would you believe, and this is one of the endearing things about Melbourne, it's still there, still exactly the same. Justin liked it. He seemed to get some of the same buzz of excitement that I did all those years ago. And I suddenly got very --- [*He searches for the word*] fearful. I wanted the best for him. I'd given him a bad start and now I desperately wanted his life to go well. I'm not trying to tell you I'm a great father, but I do care ---

PETER: Conrad, I *told* him exactly that!

CONRAD: We started to order and I told Justin that I thought it was best if I flew down to see him, rather than he come up, and suddenly he started screaming at me that I wasn't around when he really needed me so don't think I could try and make it up by flying down for a pissy lunch in a pathetic restaurant once a month. I just snapped. I got up and flew straight home. I said to myself the damage is irreparable, cut your losses or you'll ruin what's left of the rest of your life. And the situation wasn't helped by the stream of abusive letters that followed.

PETER: Conrad, I told him I was sure you loved him and that I was sure you wanted to be forgiven.

CONRAD: I wanted to be forgiven?

PETER: You did leave him when he was a year old.

CONRAD: OK it was terrible for him, but I can't spend the rest of my life apologising for a marriage that didn't work!

PETER: He said you only paid twenty dollars a week for his support.

CONRAD: [*angry*] That's a straight out lie. The sum started at twenty in the very beginning but as soon as I started to do well I adjusted and kept adjusting. You really believed that that's all I ever paid? You must have a great opinion of me!

PETER: [*trying to stay calm*] Conrad ---

CONRAD: Why didn't you at least get my side of the story!

PETER: Conrad ---

[JAQUIE *looms up behind* CONRAD.]

CONRAD: You egged him on to the point where he said things to Jaquie and I that are absolutely unforgiveable.

JAQUIE: Exactly!

CONRAD: There's no way *anyone* could pick up the pieces now!

JAQUIE: No way!

[ALEX, *lurking in the background has overheard the last part of this exchange and moves forward to replace* CONRAD.]

ALEX: What is it Peter? Suddenly you're the guru of Crystal Inlet? You know the secrets of the frigging Universe and you're gonna sock em to us whether we want em or not?

PETER: You're talking about Vicki?

ALEX: Yeah, my wife Vicki. Bordering on the edge of crazy and you tell her go for it --- Forget Alex, forget Nicholas! 747, thirteen hours, Californ-eye-ay! Yo Baby!

PETER: Alex, I told Vicki she was crazy to think of leaving you and Nicholas!

ALEX: Like hell you did. You told her she had to follow her own heart! What heart? She hasn't got a bloody heart!

PETER: Alex I said she was the only one who knew her own heart!

ALEX: Sounds like a pretty fine academic distinction to me mate!

PETER: I said the whole idea was crazy!

ALEX: That's not what she told me! Did you know Nicholas has bouts of severe depression?

PETER: No, I did not. He always seems remarkably cheerful to me. Considering.

ALEX: Yeah, well try and see beyond the surfaces occasionally before you dish out more advice!

PETER: Alex, I didn't dish out any advice.

ALEX: You told her it was perfectly O.K. to go off to the States and leave Nicholas in boarding school.

PETER: Boarding school was never mentioned!

ALEX: How the hell else is Nick gonna get any schooling if she runs out on me? How the hell am I going to cope with him on my own. I'm partner in a high pressure law firm!

PETER: Alex, I didn't say any of this!

[VICKI, *waiting in the wings, comes in on the conversation.*]

VICKI: You said I was the only one who knew my own heart.

PETER: Vicki, that is what's called a truism. It is not advice!

ALEX: You tell someone to follow their heart, that means they go!

PETER: I raised every possible objection!

ALEX: You said you can understand why she has to get out --- 'cause I'm such a bastard!

PETER: Alex, I did not ---

ALEX: How I'm cutting her down all the time. Humiliating her? Who the hell has poured good money into her bloody stupid business schemes? Me. Alex. Who the hell has let her walk all over me like a doormat all these years!

VICKI: Peter notices how you treat me. Everyone does!

ALEX: I treat you ten times better than you deserve.

PETER: Alex, I spoke to Vicki, I told her what I thought, and none of it was encouraging her to go!

VICKI: Peter, you told me to follow my heart!

ALEX: Vicki said you'd observed that Nicholas was far closer to me than her.

PETER: Alex, I did not ---

ALEX: Exactly when did you observe this?

PETER: Alex, I object to this cross examination, and ---

ALEX: Well I object to you giving half cocked advice to my wife!

INDUSTRIAL SHARE LIST
MINING AND OIL

PETER: I did not make any ---

ALEX: When have you observed this alleged closeness to Nicholas? Once or twice when Nicholas and I have been tossing a ball on the beach?

PETER: Alex ---

ALEX: [*in a rage*] Do you want to know the truth about Nicholas and I? We don't connect. And that's a real downer for me, I can tell you. I try and work out strategies to penetrate that shell of his and nothing works! I lay awake at nights worrying that this kid, who believe me I love more than anything else in this world, is still as distant from me as the moon. And I've *hated* Vicki because she connects with him without any effort.

VICKI: Alex, this is all nonsense. You're a wonderful father!

ALEX: Who does he talk to if he's got problems?

VICKI: Not me! I told you all he does is grunt!

ALEX: When he was humiliated in front of the school because of his haircut and sent home. Who talked to him for an hour and a half. Who calmed him down?

VICKI: [*crossly*] Mothers always do that sort of stuff!

ALEX: Vicki you're blind! He wasn't grunting for an hour and a half then was he? He needs you and you're about to piss off with some cretinous arsehole to the States! [*To* PETER] And you tell her to do it!

PETER: I didn't. I ---

ALEX: [*to* VICKI] I've checked Greg Hardboard out. I've been on the phone all day. He's an opportunistic sleaze who's had dozens of women over the years and if he's true to form he isn't over there setting up house for you, it's for someone considerably younger and even more stupid! [*To* PETER] And this is the guy you tell her to drop everything for?

PETER: Alex, I didn't ---

ALEX: Are you calling her a liar? The conversation didn't take place? Didn't it occur to you that Vicki is teetering on the brink of total nervous collapse and you see fit to go and encourage her! What kind of friend are you anyhow?

PETER: Alex ---

VICKI: Peter, you told me to follow my heart. You did!

ALEX: If she goes off and screws up young Nick's life I hope you'll feel pleased with yourself!

[ALEX *stands staring at him.*]

VICKI: You did Peter. You did.

[PETER *is stunned. He stands there staring at them both, then across at* CONRAD *who is still glaring at him.*]

PETER: I think I'd better go.

[*He moves towards the edge of the deck but his way is blocked by* PENNY *who has just appeared. She seems upset and angry.*]

PENNY: Peter, did you tell Stephen I was going to leave him?

PETER: No, I told him that we'd talked, and that I felt his pessimism caused you a lot of strain.

PENNY: He's in total panic. He's sure I'm just about to go again.

PETER: I'm sorry. I ---

PENNY: He's walking up and down the deck ranting.

PETER: That's one thing I've achieved. He's got a lot more confidence in its structural integrity.

PENNY: What we talked about was in confidence.

PETER: I'm sorry.

PENNY: He says you practically told him he was crazy.

PETER: I told him a lot of his fears were unnecessary.

PENNY: He's got problems. You know it and I know it, but underneath it all he's very decent person and you've reduced him to a total wreck.

[STEPHEN *is heard calling for* PENNY]

PETER: Penny, I'm really sorry.

PENNY: I *know* he can be exasperating, and there *are* times I want to give up, and it certainly hasn't been the sort of idyllic marriage you had, but we've lasted over twenty years and we've had two girls I'm really really proud of ---

PETER: [*interrupting*] Penny, I'm sorry. It was stupid and presumptuous of me, OK?

[STEPHEN *calls again for* PENNY. *She looks at* PETER *and goes.* PETER *shakes his head despairingly and leaves the deck.* MARGARET *comes out of the house.*]

MARGARET: [*to* VICKI] Sorry, I didn't mean to be on the phone so long. I left two dollars on the table. Tanya has fallen in love with a psychopath and is weeping --- God she should be shouting with joy --- weeping because he's dropped her for a gymnast. I said to her for Christ's sake isn't that just a little *suspect.* Did he ever give you a copy of the *Kama Sutra* perchance? Where's Peter?

[*Everyone shrugs and acts innocent.*]

* * *

PETER *pours some sugar into a bowl, then starts to move off towards the edge of his deck.* MARGARET *arrives and blocks his way.*

MARGARET: Where did you disappear to last night?

PETER: Have you ever seen a production of Ibsen's *The Wild Duck*?

MARGARET: No. I can't bear Lutheran guilt.

PETER: This idiot called Gregers starts telling everyone the truth because he thinks it'll be good for them. It ends up ruining everyone's lives. Conrad and Alex won't ever speak to me again and I'm not counting on any more quiche. [*He indicates the sugar bowl*] Despite massive amounts of sugar even the Lorikeets steer clear of me these days.

MARGARET: Where are you going?

PETER: To apologise to all those whose lives I've apparently ruined.

MARGARET: Has Jus --- ?

PETER: No! I haven't seen him, I don't know where he is, and I don't bloody well care!

[*He moves off then turns back.*]

My lawyers rang back.

MARGARET: Have they --- ?

INDUSTRIAL
Company
ChartMort
Chatham
Chelsea
Chew Corp
SCARLETT
GONE WITH THE WIND
MONEY

PETER: [*sarcastically*] They've been very generous. They've come down from fifty thousand to forty.

MARGARET: I'm sure Alex and Conrad and ---

PETER: After last night? Forget it!

[PETER *goes leaving* MARGARET *frowning.*]

* * *

ALEX *and* VICKI*'s deck.* ALEX *and* VICKI *are sitting reading in adjacent deckchairs, surprisingly, hand in hand. The music is again Chicago's.* It's Hard to Say I'm Sorry. ALEX *is singing along, loudly. Their hands separate as they both turn a page in the separate books they are reading.* PETER *appears on the deck. They look up.*

PETER: Sorry to interrupt. I just came to apologise ---

ALEX: As a matter of fact mate, I was coming over to apologise to you.

VICKI: [*to* PETER] As always, I interpreted what you said to suit myself.

ALEX: I'm glad you let fly mate --- it forced us to face all the big questions.

VICKI: And find out some things about each other we'd never known. I'd never dreamed Alex saw *me* as the successful parent.

ALEX: We talked it through and realised we're both bloody good parents.

VICKI: And just how important Nicholas is to both of us. I can't imagine how I ever seriously contemplated leaving him --- or Alex.

ALEX: Honey --- my fault --- If I hadn't knocked your film ambitions, there's no way you would've bonked that slime Harboard.

VICKI: It wasn't so much the infidelity --- it was my threat to go off to the States with him that was so stupid.

ALEX: Just quietly that was never going to happen. Harboard

wasn't about to cramp his style by freighting you over to Bimbo heaven.

VICKI: Alex, he wanted me with him and I was going to go ---

ALEX: You want to believe that, that's fine. The important thing is, Peter, I've still got a wife and Nick's got a mother.

VICKI: [*tersely*] Alex, don't try and minimise what happened. It was a knife edge situation that could have spelt disaster for all of us.

ALEX: Vicki, cut the drama. You screwed some nobody, and it's over. I haven't exactly been a Saint myself.

[*To* PETER]

The truth is mate I've been worse than Vicki.

VICKI: I'm sure Peter doesn't want to hear about your indiscretions as well as mine.

ALEX: I'm not about to tell him.

VICKI: Why bring it up?

ALEX: Maybe I *don't* want him to think I'm some kind of dumb cuckold, sitting round twiddling his thumbs while his wife goes out and gets laid!

VICKI: Peter, it seems Alex would like you to know that for every indiscretion of mine, he has had one also.

[*To* ALEX] Satisfied?

ALEX: For every one of yours I've had two. I just don't make it so bloody public! And I don't spill my guts to you!

VICKI: Alex, don't embarrass us both in front of Peter. I know exactly who you've slept with.

ALEX: How do you know?

VICKI: They can't keep the gleam of triumph out of their piggy little eyes.

ALEX: You don't know the half of it.

VICKI: Yes I do.

ALEX: Mona Vestian? Sarah Dufay?

VICKI: Absolutely.

ALEX: Mandy Cairncross. Five Ansett hostesses?

VICKI: [*laughs in disbelief*] Mandy Cairncross?

[ALEX *glares at her*]

ALEX: And unlike you they all had big thumping orgasms. Every one!

VICKI: Mandy Cairncross wouldn't go near you in a fit!

ALEX: Call her! [*To* PETER] Anyway mate, the important thing is that we're still together, and it's largely because you finally got us talking. Hey. I meant to tell you. I've just been made senior partner at Samuelson Bates.

PETER: Great.

ALEX: Now they're working for me instead of me working for them, and I finally crack a decent profit share for my efforts!

PETER: Congratulations.

ALEX: Come and have a drink!

[*He ushers a slightly reluctant* PETER *inside.*]

* * *

CONRAD'*s deck.* CONRAD'*s place is, as* MARGARET *warned us, huge. Certainly it has been designed to blend into the background but again we're talking big money. The music playing is Beethoven's* Ode to Joy. JUSTIN *and* CONRAD *are playing shuttlecock together, laughing and horsing around like two old friends.* JAQUIE *is watching them, cynically bemused as* PETER *walks onto the deck.*

JAQUIE: We're playing happy families.

PETER: I just came to apologise for appearing to take sides ---

CONRAD: I'm glad you did. Thanks to you it's all resolved.

PETER: Resolved?

JAQUIE: Wait for it.

CONRAD: Yep. I just didn't want to face the truth and the truth is I did dump Justin, emotionally and financially and it was high time I faced up to it and tried to make amends.

JUSTIN: Dad's been really generous, especially considering his new . . .

[*He indicates* JAQUIE'*s stomach.*]

CONRAD: Justin wants to go back to University and finish his degree and I've agreed to help him out.

JAQUIE: Conrad's just heard that the UK and Europe have bought the show and American PBS is looking good, so I guess we can afford it.

PETER: Congratulations Conrad. That's great.

CONRAD: It's not official yet, but the deal's done.

JUSTIN: International Superstar.

CONRAD: So for God's sake don't be guilty. You did us all a big favour. Come and have a drink.

[PETER *is led inside, less reluctantly this time as he is already a little drunk from the* ALEX/VICKI *reconciliation.*]

* * *

PETER *steps onto* PENNY *and* STEPHEN'*s deck. This time we definitely notice he has had a few drinks too many.* STEPHEN *is holding* PENNY'*s hand.* PETER *stops.* PENNY *turns and sees him.* STEPHEN *continues staring out to sea.*

PETER: I just came to apologise ---

PENNY: I'm sorry I got so upset Peter. Stephen and I talked things through most of last night and we realised you really meant the best for both of us.

STEPHEN: You made us realise how close to the edge our marriage really was.

PENNY: It had got to the point where hearing Stephen's voice had got to be like fingernails down a blackboard.

STEPHEN: [*excited, almost euphoric*] I realise now that my problem was fear. Deep irrational fear. It was permeating and tainting every single aspect of my life. In effect I didn't have a life because for me, all I had, every second of my waking life, was the fear. Then suddenly, at exactly three forty five this morning, I --- [*corrects himself, looks at* PENNY] We --- rolled all that fear --- [*He mimes himself vomiting up the fear*] into a tight little ball --- [*He mimes rolling the disgorged fear into a ball then with a discus hurl tosses it away*] --- and I flung it away! [*He stands there breathing deeply, standing erect*]. It's as if I've been reborn.

PENNY: All I've heard since then is optimism. It's wonderful.

STEPHEN: [*indicating the heavens*] I woke up this morning and said to myself 'How have I been missing all this? Look at the sky, the trees, the surf. Why haven't I been seeing what's there in front of my eyes?' And just as I was thinking this a whole flock of rainbow lorikeets landed right here on the deck.

PETER: [*pointing to a bowl*] Sugar?

STEPHEN: No sugar.

PETER: [*dully*] Congratulations.

PENNY: Thank you Peter. You're a real friend.

STEPHEN: To both of us.

[STEPHEN *and* PENNY *embrace.* PETER, *turns, sees the embrace, registers mild disgust and helps himself to the bottle of champagne.*]

* * *

MARGARET, CONRAD, JAQUIE, ALEX, PENNY *and* STEPHEN *are assembled around* VICKI *on her deck.*

VICKI: [*to gathering*] Thank you all for coming. I'm sorry I was so conspiratorial getting you the message, but I didn't want Peter to hear about this.

[*They look at each other wondering what this is about.*]

I've been talking to Penny and Jaquie about what's been happening lately and the three of us suddenly realised what an exceptional friend we've all got in Peter.

[*There is general and strong agreement with this statement.*]

And we started thinking that we really should do something to thank him.

[*Strong agreement.*]

We were thinking it would be nice to have a special surprise dinner in his honour down here.

[*All except* MARGARET *express strong support for this idea.*]

Alex and I would be very happy to host it.

[*All except* MARGARET *express their thanks for the offer and say they will help with the organisation.*]

ALEX: And I think it would be great if we all bought him something he'd really like. Something classy. Something expensive.

[*Again strong agreement from all except* MARGARET.]

Margaret --- you're a good friend of his. What would he *really* like?

[*All eyes on* MARGARET].

MARGARET: What would he really like?

ALEX: What would he really like?

MARGARET: [*hesitates*] Forty thousand dollars.

[*Suddenly there's dead silence.*]

[*to audience*] I promised Peter I wouldn't mention it, but there you are. I did. I told them everything.

[*There's a long silence.*]

So there you have it. I feel exactly the same way about Peter as all of you and The Inlet here is his spiritual home. Speaking personally I'd hate to lose him.

[*There's a worried nodding of heads.*]

He'd kill me if he knew I was telling you any of this, but given what he means to all of us I felt I had to speak up.

[*There's more worried nodding of heads.*]

If he wins the appeal --- and apparently there's a very good chance --- costs will be awarded and we'll all get our money back. I was going to suggest we put in ten thousand each.

ALEX: If he loses we do the lot?

MARGARET: If he loses he's virtually finished for life.

[*Pause*]

His QC is very confident he's got a strong case.

ALEX: They always are. It pays.

MARGARET: The QC says the bank definitely misinformed Peter

about the extent of the risk.

ALEX: Who's the QC?

MARGARET: Stuart Malone.

ALEX: Full on mediocrity.

JAQUIE: I can't believe anyone would sign on as guarantor without realising the dangers.

MARGARET: It was his brother.

JAQUIE: That would make me even *more* cautious.

MARGARET: I certainly wouldn't've done it for any of my relatives, but if we don't help him the rest of his life will be totally ruined.

VICKI: We've got to help. There's no question.

ALEX: Hang on, there is a question. Two questions. Chances are he'll lose the appeal, and ten thousand is a lot of dough.

MARGARET: It's hard to put a price on friendship, but for someone like Peter I think the price isn't too high.

ALEX: Don't get me wrong, he's a good guy.

VICKI: Alex, we've got to help.

ALEX: He's a good guy but the fact remains that if I had to name my twenty best friends --- to be honest he wouldn't make the list.

[*There's a murmur of protest at this statement.*]

VICKI: Alex, you haven't got twenty friends. If we leave out the desperates you've bonked we couldn't be talking more than two or three.

ALEX: We go to dinner parties at the rate of dozens a week. I got friends coming out my ears. Has Peter ever come to our place in the city? Ever? Once?

MARGARET: Have any of us?

VICKI: Alex, don't do this. There's a special friendship down here we all share and Peter's at the hub of it.

ALEX: Vicki, you're talking shit. Not two weeks ago you said we should sell up here and buy in Palm Beach because more of our friends were there.

[*The others look at each other, hurt and angry.*]

VICKI: [*embarrassed*] It was only the vaguest of possibilities.

CABLE BAY

ALEX: [*angry, guilty*] Look, I'm not saying he's not a good guy. I'm just trying to strip away the sentimentality and bullshit because there's ten thousand dollars involved here that we're most likely never going to see again.

VICKI: Alex, we're going to help!

ALEX: Vicki, I'd like to help the homeless kids on the street, I'd like to help the pensioners who can't pay their heating bills. The world's a tough place. There are guys bleeding from the ears all over the country 'cause of this recession we're in. There are farmers walking off their land in droves with nowhere to go! It's hell in a heatwave out there!

VICKI: Alex we could ---

ALEX: [*interrupting*] You want me to go and ring up and cancel the boat? After waiting ten years for something decent instead of the little twenty foot toy we've got up there now? What's the use of a bloody waterfront if we can't even use it?

VICKI: Would it mean cancelling the boat?

ALEX: Yes! I'm stretched to the limit!

MARGARET: Quite frankly Alex, I thought you'd have less problems raising it than any of us. I'm going to have to take out a mortgage.

ALEX: Margaret, I've been working my guts out for that boat.

VICKI: [*to* MARGARET] It has been something he's wanted very very much.

CONRAD: What size Alex?

ALEX: Fifty two footer. Ocean going. Eight berth. The real thing.

PENNY: You're going to mortgage your house Margaret?

MARGARET: [*nodding*] Don't get me wrong. I'm not delighted to be doing it --- but I can't ask all of you without offering myself.

PENNY: We could afford it Stephen.

STEPHEN: [*almost rigid with terror*] How? The only cushion we've got against our old age are the property investments. Every spare cent I earn is earmarked. I can't keep working to 65 like Joe Blow. Do you know the strain involved in surgery? They've done electrocardiograms on surgeons hearts and sometimes the stress is twice as great as a pilot landing an F18.

PENNY: [*irritated*] That was surgeons doing open heart. You don't have to get *bones* beating again.

STEPHEN: Penny, I've got heart irregularities, colitis, skin problems, and a defective kidney --- all of them stress related. If I had to stop work now our income level from our investments would barely get us through.

PENNY: Your property investments are returning way over a thousand dollars a week clear!

STEPHEN: If something happened to me tomorrow that's all we'd have to live on! How could we live on a thousand a week?

PENNY: Stephen --- Fear? You weren't going to let it dominate your life any more? Remember?

STEPHEN: [*fearfully*] This has nothing to do with fear! Immediate family in genuine distress have some call on your resources, but not friends.

PENNY: Who made up that rule?

CONRAD: Interestingly it has a deep genetic basis.

MARGARET: [*warning*] Conrad.

CONRAD: A blood relative shares some of our own genes --- and when we help that relative, we're in a sense helping our own genetic immortality. No matter how much we *like* Peter our lack of shared genes makes us feel a deep level resistance.

JAQUIE: Conrad, there's no need to get theoretical about this. The practical fact is you've just pledged money to your prodigal son to the tune of well over ten thousand dollars and that's our charity budget for the year.

CONRAD: If I was certain my International deal was going ahead I'd be much more willing to consider it.

MARGARET: [*terse*] I know I'm asking a lot, but could you all just focus for a second on what's going to happen to Peter if we *don't* help.

ALEX: Margaret, what's happened to Peter is a full on bummer but these are hard times all over.

MARGARET: Alex, wasn't there some talk about you becoming the Senior Partner at Samuelson Bates.

ALEX: Nothing's been finalised.

[He gives VICKI *a threatening glance indicating that she better not correct him.]*

PENNY: Stephen, you know we can afford it.

STEPHEN: *[almost hysterical]* No! I said no!

VICKI: Alex, are you *sure* it would mean we couldn't get the boat?

ALEX: Yes! What do you think? I shit money?

MARGARET: I can't believe I'm hearing this. I'm putting in ten thousand. Who's going to match it?

[She looks at each couple in turn. PENNY *can't budge* STEPHEN, ALEX *and* VICKI *stand firm.* CONRAD *steps forward as if he might relent but is stopped by an 'uh uh' from* JAQUIE. *There is a silence.]*

* * *

MARGARET*'s deck.* PETER *comes onstage carrying* Possession. *He calls out but she is not home. He notices* JUSTIN*'s backpack.* MARGARET *appears on the deck and walks up to him and gives him a warm consoling embrace.*

PETER: Hi.

MARGARET: Hi. I told them.

PETER: What?

MARGARET: About your situation.

PETER: *[shocked]* Margaret. You promised you wouldn't.

MARGARET: Sorry.

PETER: Margaret, this is really embarrassing. They'll assume I told you to tell them.

MARGARET: I assured them you didn't.

PETER: You didn't mention money?

MARGARET: I asked them to put in ten thousand each.

PETER: Margaret, I mightn't be able to pay them back.

MARGARET: You won't have to. They refused.

[PETER *is shocked to hear this but tries to disguise it.*]

Do you know what prompted me to ask them? They were organising a surprise party to thank you for helping them all! I'm so angry I can hardly speak. I *know* they could all manage it without any trouble!

[*There's a pause.* PETER *stares ahead, still in semi shock.*]

I couldn't believe the excuses. Conrad's scared his contract won't be renewed ---

PETER: It has been.

[MARGARET *looks at him.*]

Jaquie told me. They've sold into Europe and probably the States. And Alex's just been made senior partner.

MARGARET: You're joking!

PETER: Alex told me himself.

MARGARET: The bastards!

[*There's a pause.*]

PETER: They all just said no. Straight away?

MARGARET: No, not straight away.

PETER: They did consider it?

MARGARET: For about five minutes. Penny was the only one who wanted to do it, but she was well and truly torpedoed by Dr. Gloom.

PETER: No one else?

MARGARET: [*nodding*] Vicki showed a flutter of enthusiasm until Alex made her face the full horror of another summer without a fifty-two foot boat. Alex simply redefined you as a distant acquaintance.

PETER: Conrad?

MARGARET: Conrad seemed to be wavering, until he caught the glint of the pregnant piranha's teeth.

[JUSTIN *comes onto her deck. She stares at him.*]

You've finally deigned to come and see me?

JUSTIN: Sorry. I've been working things out with Dad.

[PETER *retreats off the deck to give them some privacy.*]

MARGARET: So what was the outcome of that?

JUSTIN: He's paying for me to finish Uni. I thought I'd stay in Sydney and finish it there.

MARGARET: [*nodding*] Good.

JUSTIN: He said I'd had the roughest deal of any of his kids, and that letting me do what I wanted to do for three years of my life was the least he could do by way of compensation. I couldn't believe my ears.

MARGARET: He's one of the most self obsessed men I've ever met, but there's a corner of him somewhere that loves you.

JUSTIN: I cried. I didn't let him see me but I went away and cried.

[*Pause*]

MARGARET: Do you want to stay with me --- back in the city --- until you work out what you want to do?

JUSTIN: [*shamefaced*] Well that's er, very kind but er ---

[*Tense pause.*]

MARGARET: [*nodding*] I'm old enough to be your mother.

JUSTIN: I know it shouldn't worry me, but ---

[*Pause.*]

It wouldn't work for you either. You *do* think everything I say is a cliché.

MARGARET: [*an outpouring*] Justin I've spent so much time refining my intellect and tastes that just about everything I hear from everyone is a cliché. The only people who *really* interest me are a handful of authors and social commentators who I'm never likely to meet in my life.

JUSTIN: That's pretty sad.

MARGARET: [*meaning it*] Yes it is.

JUSTIN: Margaret, I think you're really --- [*a terrific person*]

MARGARET: Don't say anything Justin, just go.

[JUSTIN *moves away.*]

Got your backpack?

[JUSTIN *stops, comes back and takes his backpack and goes.* PETER *comes back.*]

PETER: What happened?

MARGARET: No deal.

PETER: He's a nice kid, but you said yourself you weren't exactly planning to marry him.

MARGARET: I'm old enough to be his mother.

[*Pause*]

PETER: I just finished A.S. Byatt. I liked it. Maud Bailey is a bit like you.

MARGARET: [*narrowly*] Breathtakingly beautiful? Six foot tall?

PETER: In her intellectual range and . . . [*searches for the word*]

MARGARET: Arrogance?

PETER: Sense of her own worth.

MARGARET: Peter, I'm lending you the forty thousand.

[PETER *stares at her.*]

I am Peter. Even if I have to stuff the cash through your letter box.

PETER: Where would you get the money?

MARGARET: A mortgage on my house. Look I'm not crazy. I've been ringing round every lawyer I know and they think you're going to win the appeal.

PETER: There's too much risk.

MARGARET: Peter, it's being done for totally selfish motives. This is the only place in the world I love to be, and you're my very special friend and I want you here.

[PETER *stares at her.*]

[*picking up* Possession] I *did* identify with Maud Bailey. When Roland got through that prickly exterior, he found it was just a survival mechanism. What she wanted was what most of us want. Acceptance, love.

[PETER *is momentarily at a loss for words.*]

PETER: Margaret I definitely can't have you mortgaging ---

MARGARET: [*angrily*] Peter just accept it! It'll cost me a bit over a hundred and twenty dollars a week, and for God's sake I can live with that for a year or so.

PETER: I might lose the appeal.

MARGARET: You won't lose the appeal! I'll sit in the courtroom and stare down the Judge!

[MARGARET *can't speak. There are tears running down*

her cheeks. PETER *goes across and puts his arm around her.*]

PETER: Why are you so upset?

MARGARET: Tourists were very safe for me. I could keep believing they didn't leave me because they wanted to. It was just that they had to go home. I could keep believing I was still as magnetically alluring as I was at twenty-five.

[*Pause*]

Encounters with mirrors at my age are carefully pre planned. Lighting right. Angles right. But sometimes you accidently catch sight of yourself in a glass shopfront and the fantasy's over.

[*Pause*]

I won't be prowling the galleries any more.

[*Pause*]

It would have been a very neat solution if you and I ...

PETER: Yes, I've thought ...

MARGARET: Really?

PETER: I've always found you very attractive.

MARGARET: But?

PETER: You've got a certain er, force of --- [*personality*] ---

MARGARET: [*nodding. She has heard this phrase before*] Personality.

[*Pause*]

I've always *liked* you enormously, but I thought you were a little too --- gooey at the centre.

PETER: Ah.

MARGARET: Too nice.

[*Pause*]

Aren't you angry at those bastards?

PETER: Yes.

MARGARET: Let them know it!

PETER: What's the use?

MARGARET: To make them feel guilty! To make them squirm!

PETER: Vindictiveness doesn't really achieve anything.

MARGARET: Yes it does. It makes you feel great!

[PETER *stares at her. The tears still run down her cheeks but her manner is totally emphatic.*]

* * *

CONRAD'*s deck.* CONRAD, JAQUIE, VICKI, ALEX, PENNY, STEPHEN, *and* JUSTIN *are sipping drinks. The music playing is a full throated mass choir doing Handel's* Messiah.

ALEX: It's been a great holiday. Weather, everything.

CONRAD: The only sour note, of course, is what's happened to Peter.

[*There's general agreement that this has been a downer. There's an awkward silence. Heads turn as* PETER *and* MARGARET *appear on the deck.*]

VICKI: [*embarrassed*] Peter, Margaret.

PETER: I'm sorry. I didn't realise you were entertaining.

JAQUIE: [*Lying*] Peter, you're more than welcome. I was looking around for you on the beach to invite you both up.

PETER: I'm glad I caught you all up here. I was going to come around and see you all individually. I was *extraordinarily* embarrassed that Margaret took it on herself to ask you for money on my account.

MARGARET: Peter had asked me not to even mention his financial situation. I'm sorry.

[*There are cries of protest.*]

CONRAD: We're really sorry we couldn't help.

[*There's strong agreement with this statement.*]

PETER: I didn't expect you to. It was my own fault. I should never have agreed to go guarantor. And I think what Margaret has done is totally bizarre.

CONRAD: What's she done?

PETER: She's taking out a mortgage to lend me the whole forty thousand. I think she's crazy and I've told her, but she's doing it.

[*The others look at each other in semi shock.*]

I just wanted to assure you that if I win the appeal, that as far as I'm concerned you're all still my friends.

[*The friends look at each other guiltily.*]

I have to admit that my first reaction was to say 'Bugger the lot of you,' but then I remembered the companionship, the fun, and the confidences we'd shared.

[*He pauses, looking at them.*]

Stephen. The moment you told me how you'd thrown away your fear. [*He mimes Stephen vomiting up his fear*] How many moments like that do you share with your friends?

[*He smiles at* STEPHEN, *walks away and mutters 'dork!' He moves across to* ALEX].

And Alex. I felt really privileged that night you told me how your conscience was ripping you apart. Really privileged.

ALEX: I don't remember that.

PETER: You were very drunk, but very, very honest. [*To the others*] He was very tough on himself.

ALEX: What did I say?

PETER: You told me in confidence.

ALEX: What did I say?

PETER: You said you'd prostituted your legal skills to help our big entrepreneurs rip off their investors.

[*He smiles at* ALEX *and as he moves away mutters 'harlot'. He heads towards* VICKI.]

And Vicki, you were just as honest.

VICKI: [*alarmed*] When?

PETER: That same night. You told me that if you *didn't* get your photo in the social pages at least once a month you went into total depression.

[*He smiles at her and as he moves away he mutters 'leech.'*]

But it hasn't been all gloom. There's been such a lot of laughter here over the years. You had me helpless one night on this deck Jaquie. Remember?

JAQUIE: [*tersely*] No.

PETER: The list?

JAQUIE: What list?

PETER: You told me that when you couldn't stand journalism any longer you drew up a hit list of twenty shakily married wealthy men and Conrad was number nineteen. [*Sudden apparent concern*] You've told him this haven't you?

JAQUIE: [*tersely*] No.

PETER: Sorry, I assumed you had. Conrad, I can *assure* you she said it in the sense that while things started out as expedient, she was surprised how much she'd grown to love you. Truly.

[*He moves away from* CONRAD *and mutters 'sperm bank!'*]

VICKI: Alex and I had better be going, Jaquie.

STEPHEN: Yes, we were just about to go too.

[*They start to shuffle off, but are headed off by* PETER.]

PETER: Please. I don't want anyone to be embarrassed on my account. I truly didn't expect any of you to subsidise my stupidity. Truly. Congratulations on your promotion Alex. About time they paid you what you were worth. You too Conrad. Good to know the rest of the world is going to get you soon. There was a report of the deal in this morning's paper.

CONRAD: That sum quoted is the production company fees. I only get a small proportion of that.

PETER: Of course. I just popped in for a second. I'm glad I saw you all and please, please don't be embarrassed. I'll see you all around.

[*He pats* STEPHEN *on the shoulder, repeats his mime of* STEPHEN *vomiting up his fear, and moves off with* MARGARET *who remembers something and turns.*]

MARGARET: Oh. Justin. When do you want to collect those things you left at my place in the city?

[CONRAD *stares at* JUSTIN.]

[*to* CONRAD] Justin and I are, sorry were, lovers. And Justin, I just want you to know that as far as I'm concerned there are no hard feelings. It was great.

[*She goes across and kisses him on the cheek, watched by*

a horrified CONRAD, *then follows* PETER *off the deck. The guests look at each other.* CONRAD *stares at* JUSTIN *who becomes uncomfortable and angry.*]

JUSTIN: She's twenty years older than me, you're twenty years older than Jaquie. What's the problem?

CONRAD: The male being older makes evolutionary sense! The women gets proven genes!

JUSTIN: Only while the old guy can still get it up.

[*He walks back into the house.*]

STEPHEN: Forty thousand dollars? Has she gone crazy?

ALEX: It's gonna make us look like absolute arseholes when the word gets around.

VICKI: I wanted to help, but you said we'd lose the boat!

ALEX: All right, I'm sorry. You want to give him the money, we'll give him the money. He probably will win the bloody appeal.

STEPHEN: [*terrified*] Oh, Jesus. Don't start this again!

ALEX: [*burst of enthusiasm*] You know what I reckon? Let's cut Miss Smart Knickers outa the whole deal. Wipe that smug look off her face. I can go fifteen. Conrad?

CONRAD: Fifteen?

ALEX: Stephen goes ten and we cut her out of the whole action!
[*He dances on the balls of his feet like a boxer*]
Let's just see how she handles that?

PENNY: I don't think the point of the exercise is to be vindictive Alex.

ALEX: She only did it for the brownie points. Stuff her!

CONRAD: Fifteen?

JAQUIE: Just a minute.

ALEX: The odds are he's gonna win the appeal and we'll get our money back anyhow.

JAQUIE: That's not what you said yesterday!

ALEX: The banks are losing two out of every three of these. Three outa every four.

CONRAD: You're sure?

ALEX: It's an eighty twenty chance his way. Let's take a punt.

CONRAD: OK. Fifteen.
STEPHEN: [*terror struck*] No way!
PENNY: Stephen --- No more fear --- remember?
STEPHEN: [*savagely*] Penny, keep *out* of this! This is money! This is different!
ALEX: Stephen, you're a bloody wimp. I'll go twenty.
CONRAD: Eighty twenty he'll win?
ALEX: Absolutely. Believe me buddy!
CONRAD: OK twenty.
JAQUIE: Conrad!
CONRAD: Just shut up! It's my money! If you don't like it go and marry number twenty!
ALEX: [*shaking hands with* CONRAD] Done! Hey I feel great. For once in my life I'm the good guy.
VICKI: Remember the moment. It's not likely to happen again.
ALEX: [*loud, exuberant*] Get me a drink! A toast to the good guys!
STEPHEN: You're both crazy. Absolutely crazy!
ALEX: Slope off wimp! Go find a retirement village!

[ALEX *turns his back on* STEPHEN. PENNY, *disgusted with her husband moves off.* STEPHEN *stands there stunned and isolated as the two 'good guys' toast themselves. Handel's* Messiah *swells to a thunderous crescendo.*]

* * *

MARGARET'*s deck. She is standing in the sunlight looking down at the waves below.* PETER *comes up onto the deck. The music is another of Bach's Brandenburg concertos.*

PETER: Hi.
MARGARET: Hi.
PETER: You don't need to mortgage anything.

[MARGARET *stares at him.*]

Conrad and Alex were just up on my deck writing out two cheques for twenty thousand each.

[MARGARET *stares at him.*]

I think I'm going to be vindictive more often.

MARGARET: They've covered the lot?

PETER: [*nodding*] Thank God you're off the hook.

[PENNY *comes onto the deck from the other side.* PETER *and* MARGARET *greet her.*]

PENNY: They've given you the cheques?

PETER: Yeah. Whatever their motives they're taking a hell of risk and I appreciate it.

PENNY: I just want to say that I'm deeply ashamed of Stephen's behaviour, and that if I had any money of my own, you'd have it.

PETER: Penny, you're one person who *doesn't* need to buy my friendship. Truly.

PENNY: I'm leaving Stephen. All that euphoria about a new start was rubbish. He's a gutless human being and he's going to stay that way.

MARGARET: Penny, there are just two words I want to say. About time.

PENNY: I should have done it years ago. I guess I won't be coming down here to Crystal Inlet any more but I hope we can still be friends.

[PETER *and* MARGARET *affirm that they will.*]

All the best in the appeal Peter. I'd better go.

MARGARET: Penny, if you ever want to come down here and stay in this place ---

PETER: Or mine. If I win the appeal.

[*Pause*]

If I'm not using it.

PENNY: Thank you. Both of you. I'll be in touch.

[*She goes.* MARGARET *turns to* PETER *and raises her eyebrows.*]

PETER: Margaret stop it. She hasn't even *left* him yet.

MARGARET: She's going to. She meant it.

PETER: Margaret. Just because she brought me a few quiches doesn't mean she wants to share my life.

MARGARET: I've got a very strong intuition about you two.
PETER: The first thing on my agenda is the court appeal.
MARGARET: [*to audience*] Peter won his appeal, plus costs, so Alex and Conrad got their money back. [STEPHEN *appears onstage*] Stephen sold his house at the Inlet and married a beautiful nursing sister from the Philippines who is currently using most of his money to import the rest of her vast family. If you thought he was gloomy at the Inlet, you should see him now. [ALEX *appears*] Alex got his fifty-two foot boat but at the start of the Sydney Hobart yacht race collided with a Maxi Yacht and is in heavy litigation. [VICKI *appears*] Vicki started a small local film production company funded by guess who, and is currently trying to raise finance for an eco romance which combines the greenhouse effect with torrid sex. [CONRAD *and* JAQUIE *appear*] Conrad and Jaquie are the proud parents of little Jake, a true horror who got the worst genes from both of them. [JUSTIN *appears*] Justin is getting honours in literature and no doubt deeply in love with some simpering little nitwit. My emotional life? Remember Naomi in Sociology? I've started a relationship of sorts with her estranged husband. My intuition about Peter and Penny? [PENNY *appears*] Penny is living with a beautiful young sculptor, with an alcohol problem, whom she's trying to rehabilitate, [PETER *appears*] and Peter is having a torrid affair with a married friend of Claudia's who is known, quite frankly, as a bit of a tart. He's racked with guilt, but then, as we frequently remark to each other, life's patterns are seldom neat. One giant plus, as far as both of us are concerned, is that we're still very good friends.

[MARGARET *rejoins* PETER *as they begin to play scrabble. The Brandenburg concerto swells. The lights fade.*]

THE END.

Also from Currency

The Retreat of Our National Drama

Julian Meyrick

Currency House Platform Paper No. 39, May 2014

To Meyrick, we have surrendered our Australian dramatic consciousness. This Paper is not about defending Tennessee Williams over David Williamson, but about understanding the specific needs of our national drama.

Making new work is hard primary research. To succeed, we need a dedicated national theatre, says Meyrick; a co-commissioning, co-production house that will address seriously the developement of new Australian drama—and the construction of our own classic repertoire.

For more information visit: www.currencyhouse.org.au

Make it Australian

Gabrielle Wolf

The Australian Performing Group, or APG, helped to bring about a profound change in Australian theatre and nurtured the talents of a generation of writers and performers who have become household names including Max Gillies, David Williamson, Graeme Blundell, Jack Hibberd, Sue Ingleton and Greig Pickhaver (aka H G Nelson).

Make it Australian gives an outsider's view of this influential group and the social, political and cultural context in which it operated.

To view our full catalogue visit:
www.currency.com.au

Currency Press • Sydney